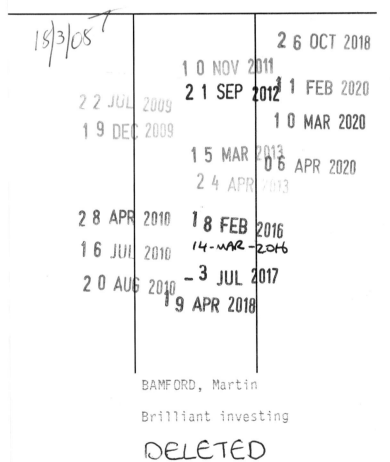

15/3/05

26 OCT 2018

10 NOV 2011

21 SEP 2012 1 FEB 2020

22 JUL 2009

19 DEC 2009   10 MAR 2020

15 MAR 2013
06 APR 2020
24 APR 2013

28 APR 2010   18 FEB 2016

16 JUL 2010   14-MAR-2016

20 AUG 2010 -3 JUL 2017
9 APR 2018

brilliant

investing

What the best investors know, do and say

Martin Bamford

PEARSON
Prentice Hall

Harlow, England • London • New York • Boston • San Francisco • Toronto • Sydney • Singapore • Hong Kong
Tokyo • Seoul • Taipei • New Delhi • Cape Town • Madrid • Mexico City • Amsterdam • Munich • Paris • Milan

PEARSON EDUCATION LIMITED

Edinburgh Gate
Harlow CM20 2JE
Tel: +44 (0) 1279 623623
Fax: +44 (0) 1279 431059
Website: www.pearsoned.co.uk

First edition published in Great Britain 2008

ISBN: 987-0-273-71483-5

British Library Cataloguing-in-Publication Data
A catalogue record for this book is available from the British Library

Library of Congress Cataloging-in-Publiction Data
A catalog record for this book is available from the Library of Congress

10 9 8 7 6 5 4 3 2 1
11 10 09 08 07

Typeset in 10/1⁄
Printed and boı

The publisher's

Gosport

ıle forests.

About the author

Martin Bamford has been an investment adviser for five years and is joint managing director of professional advisory firm Informed Choice Ltd (**www.informedchoice.ltd.uk**). At only 28 he already holds the Advanced Financial Planning Certificate from the Chartered Insurance Institute (CII). He is an Associate of the Personal Finance Society and an Associate of the Institute of Financial Planning.

Martin's first book, *The Money Tree*, was published in 2006 by Pearson Education and became the WH Smith Business Book of the Month. He is no stranger to the media, writing for *FS Focus*, *Canary Wharf City Life*, *Money Marketing* and IFAonline. He is regularly quoted in the national press, including the *Telegraph*, the *Observer*, *The Times* and the *Independent*. In his capacity as a financial expert, Martin has been a regular guest on BBC and commercial radio.

In September 2006, Martin was named as one of the most influential independent financial advisers in Britain by *Professional Adviser* magazine. His firm, Informed Choice, is one of only two IFAs in the UK to receive the Gold Standard for Independent Financial Advice at the Gold Standard Awards 2006. In January 2007 Martin was a finalist for IFA Personality of the Year at the Professional Adviser Awards.

Martin lives in Surrey with his wife and their baby daughter. In his spare time he enjoys walking in the countryside, scuba-diving and fly-fishing.

Contents

Acknowledgements

Firstly, a big thank you must go to my wife Lindie for her continued support and encouragement. This book could not have happened without you.

Special thanks to our daughter Megan who motivates and inspires me to succeed in everything I do.

Thank you to Sam Jackson, Liz Kelly and all of the team at Pearson Education for turning my reasonable words into a wonderful book.

I would also like to thank my clients and colleagues for their support during the creation of this book.

Thank you all.

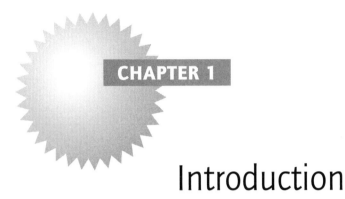

CHAPTER 1

Introduction

Have you ever wanted to invest money but just left it in your deposit account because doubt crept in? Have you ever invested money and wondered if you made the right decision? Have you ever reviewed your investments at the end of the year and wondered if they did as well as they could do?

Brilliant investing gives you all the confidence and information you need to make the most of your money. It will ensure that every investment decision you make is a brilliant one *and* show you that investing money does not need to be complex and risky. It is often said that a little bit of knowledge can be dangerous – when you are making investment decisions a little bit of knowledge is essential but a lot of knowledge is preferable.

brilliant tip

When it comes to money, the more you know the faster it will grow.

This book will not replace the professional advice and guidance you should always seek from an appropriately qualified and regulated adviser. That does not mean the investment tips you get from the chap down the pub or a girlfriend on the golf course. Everyone has their own views when it comes to investing money. Unless that person is authorised and regulated by the

> you should remember it is only advice and not an instruction

Financial Services Authority (more on that later) those views need to be taken with a shovel full of salt. Even if the individual is a regulated adviser you should remember it is only advice and not an instruction.

Getting the most from this book

This book can be a valuable aid to your investment decision-making process. But it is just a start.

- Use this book to build a strong foundation of investment knowledge before taking any risk with your money.
- Use this book in conjunction with wider reading about different investments and professional advice from regulated advisers.
- Use this book as a source of reference when you need to find out more about a particular investment option.
- Whatever you do, use this book!

You can read this book from start to finish or, if you prefer, dip in from time to time when you need some specific guidance. Each chapter starts with an explanation of what you can expect to find there and what you will learn. At the end of each chapter you will find a short summary for when you need a quick refresher.

Finding your way around this book

Investments are tough enough without trying to find your way around a book on investing that makes your life any tougher. Here is what you will find in this book.

Chapter 2: Investing basics

This chapter looks at the basics of investing your money. It will explain why you should bother to invest your money in the first place. With 'risk free' returns from cash many people will wonder why they need to take risks with their money (and pay for the privilege!) when it can sit safely in the bank or building society. Within this chapter we also take a closer look at what returns you can expect to get from your investments and the things you need to consider before investing your money.

Chapter 3: Risk and reward

This chapter is all about risk and reward. Unless you have been living on another planet you will have seen the risk warnings that accompany adverts for investments. This chapter will translate these risk warnings down into plain English so you can understand how investment risk works. More importantly, it takes a closer look at the very special relationship between investment risk, reward and volatility, the up and down movements of a particular investment.

Chapter 4: Places to invest your money

The fourth chapter looks at all of the places you might consider investing your money. Starting with stocks and shares we look at how these work, where to find more information about company shares and how to trade in this type of investment. This chapter also demystifies property investment, setting out the basics for property investment before revealing some of the secrets associated with this asset class. We also look at fixed interest securities and cash within this chapter, in order to cover the four main asset classes.

Chapter 5: Alternative investments

This chapter is all about alternative investments and what to watch out for when considering some of the more 'exotic' investment options. These include wine, art, gold, antiques and hedge funds. Whilst these investments would not normally make up a large part of an overall portfolio they can add some excitement to a larger basket of investments.

Chapter 6: Tax and investments

Investing money usually leads to a tax bill! Chapter 6 is all about the impact of tax on your investments. It explains how different investments are taxed and how to avoid, or at least minimise, your tax bill when investing money.

Chapter 7: Becoming a brilliant investor

Without a clear investment strategy, you are doomed to a poor or mediocre experience when investing money. To be a brilliant investor, you need to have a brilliant investment strategy. Chapter 7 explores five brilliant investment strategies which are all designed to reduce risk and improve your chances of getting excellent returns.

> to be a brilliant investor, you need to have a brilliant investment strategy

Chapter 8: Get advice

The eighth chapter is all about investment advice – where to find it, what you should pay for it and what to expect from an ongoing relationship with an investment adviser; not just any investment adviser but a brilliant adviser.

Chapter 9: Brilliant do's and don'ts

There are plenty of do's and don'ts when it comes to investing your money. Chapter 9 looks at a series of classic investment mistakes and helps you to spot the signs that an investment is unsuitable for you.

Chapter 10: Brilliant tips

The final chapter contains ten tips to ensure that every investment decision you make is a brilliant investment decision.

A plea from the author

Make this book your own. You paid for it so you should use it and get lots of value from it. As an author there is nothing worse than finding a used copy of your book that still looks brand new. Make notes, underline sections, fold the corners of pages. Whatever you do, use this book!

> whatever you do, use this book!

If anything in this book is unclear and you have read it twice, I apologise profusely. I am a great believer in plain English and keeping things simple. Unfortunately investments do not always play by the same rules. Where I have had to use jargon I have always tried to add a *brilliant definition* to help you along.

Finally, if you like what you find in the rest of this book please do not keep it a secret. The more people that read this book, the more people will become brilliant investors and we should all be just a bit happier. Do go and tell your friends, family and colleagues that you have discovered a brilliant book about becoming a brilliant investor.

Enjoy!

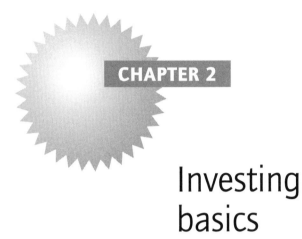

CHAPTER 2

Investing
basics

To become a brilliant investor you need to have a great understanding of the basics of investing. This chapter is all about the basics. By the end of it you will understand why you should bother investing money in the first place, what sort of return you can expect from different investments and the things you need to consider before you invest your money.

brilliant definition

Investing is all about making money grow – getting the best return on your investments without taking excessive risks.

But before you become a brilliant investor, you need to understand the basics. These are the fundamental building blocks for investment that will ensure your portfolio has a solid foundation. Get these basics wrong and every investment decision you make will be doomed to failure. I don't mean to sound melodramatic, but that's the size of the matter! Failing

> get these basics wrong and every investment decision you make will be doomed

to put the investment building blocks in place will leave you with a hit or miss investment strategy. Sometimes things might work out well but that will be down more to luck than judgement. Later in this chapter we take a look at some basic investment mistakes. By reading about such mistakes you will know how to avoid them.

brilliant tip

Learning the investing basics will enable you to make better decisions, avoid bad investment choices and invest your hard-earned cash with confidence.

The building blocks for a brilliant investor

Before you become a brilliant investor you need to understand three important investment concepts. The first – compounding – was considered by Albert Einstein to be the 'eighth wonder of the world'. That's arguable, but it is certainly a very important investment concept. The other two concepts are equally important if you are to understand the way your investments are likely to behave.

1 Compounding

Einstein got so excited about this investment concept because it shows how investments can grow at a much faster rate. Compounding describes the way that investment growth is added to investments and then new returns are based on the original investment and the growth. As time goes by and more growth is added, the investment gets larger at a much faster rate.

brilliant example

Imagine that you have £1,000 to invest and you get an investment return of 5% each year. If you took this growth out of the investment each year the total value of the investment (and the growth you had taken out) would be £1,500 after ten years. Not a bad return over ten years, but now look what happens if you leave the growth invested and allow it to 'compound'. After ten years the compounded return would be £1,628 – a whopping £128 more just because you left the growth invested.

2 Pound cost averaging

If you have money to invest it could make sense to invest it gradually – say monthly – rather than in a lump sum. This is because some months you will be buying the investment when it is expensive and other months you will be buying when it is cheap. Over time you will be investing at the average price of the investment. This is known as pound cost averaging.

Pound cost averaging is a way of avoiding the risk that you are investing when the markets are too high. It is also a way of making sure you get to buy a larger quantity of a specific investment when the markets are cheap. Because it is difficult to judge when a market is high or low, this is a very simple way of making sure you get best value.

Not everyone agrees that pound cost averaging is a good thing. Some argue that if you have cash to invest today it is better invested for a longer term than gradually drip-fed into investments over time. This is because you might miss out on a rising investment if you take your time over investing.

Whether you agree with this concept or not, it is a good way of reducing risk if you are a regular investor.

3 The time value of money (impact of price inflation)

This is an investment concept that suggests it is better to have a sum of money in your hands today than the same amount at some point in the future. Because things get more expensive to

> it is better to have £100 today than £100 tomorrow

buy over time, as a result of inflation, it is better to have £100 today than £100 tomorrow.

You also miss out on the opportunity to invest the money if you wait to receive it in the future. Even if you just put the money in a savings account you could make it grow and end up with more than if you received the same amount in the future. This is a double-whammy because as well as inflation reducing the value of the money in the future you miss out on the potential for some investment growth.

So, if you are ever offered £100 today or £100 in ten years' time, you know what to say.

Avoid the basic investment mistakes

If you know what the basic investment mistakes look like you are far less likely to make them yourself. Learn from the basic mistakes made by other investors and you will stand a far better chance of becoming a brilliant investor.

Here are five classic investment mistakes I see being made on a frequent basis.

1 Following past winners and expecting the same results

You will already be familiar with the classic investment risk warning 'past performance is no guarantee of future performance'. Yet many investors completely ignore this when making investment decisions. The simple fact is that returns from individual investment funds are rarely repeated in any consistent manner. Picking the top performing investment fund this year is the short cut to being invested in a poorly performing fund next year.

The next time you see that risk warning, take the advice! We do not use this risk warning for fun. It is factual because past performance is no guide to what might happen to the investment in the future. Just because an investment has returned 20% over the past 12 months is no guarantee it will do the same again this year.

2 Investing for the short term

This is almost always a big mistake as it does not allow enough time for your portfolio to recover if and when things go wrong. If you have a short investment term of less than three to five years, then stick to cash. This is a golden rule and one you should never forget.

It is not worth exposing your money to the risk of capital loss if you do not have the time for it to recover before you need access to the cash again. However tempting the short-term returns from an investment might look, you must always consider the length of time you have left until you need to get your hands on the cash.

> always consider the length of time you have left

One year is rarely enough time for an investment to recover once it has crashed. Two years is not much better. If you can afford to wait three years or longer, you might start to consider an investment. Any less than this and you should stick with cash.

3 Putting all of your investment eggs in a single basket

Failing to spread risk, or diversify, is a classic basic investment mistake. When all of your money is exposed to a single investment you will lose a lot of money if things go wrong.

By spreading your money around you stand a much better chance that some of your investments will perform well if others are performing badly. This makes the overall investment returns much more acceptable, whilst one set of returns in isolation is more likely to be disappointing.

4 Not taking enough risk

Not taking enough risk is another basic investment mistake. By taking too little risk you can miss out on the potential for greater returns over the long term. Whilst it is important to invest in line with your comfort levels, it is also important to give your money the chance to grow.

If you are investing for the very long term (for example, when investing within a pension fund for retirement) you can afford to take more risk than you can with shorter-term investments. Taking more risk and things going wrong is less of a problem if your investments have plenty of time to recover. This is why risk should be linked to the term of your investments. We cover this in more detail in the next chapter.

5 Relying on your own home as an investment

Property prices have been growing at a steady rate for years in the UK. Whilst this makes a great topic for dinner party conversation it does not make you a brilliant investor. Experts have different views about the role of the main residence in an investment portfolio. Many would argue that, as you cannot easily get your hands on cash unless you sell your house, it should be excluded from your financial objectives when it comes to investment.

> your home is not usually an investment. It is a place to live

Your home is not usually an investment. It is a place to live. When your house goes up in value, so do other houses. Most people cannot simply sell up and take the cash from the value of their house because they need a roof over their heads.

Three things to always consider

There are three things you need to do every time you make an investment. Do these three things every time and you will be well on your way to becoming a brilliant investor. The three crucial brilliant investment actions are – research, plan and review.

Research

When it comes to making a brilliant investment, the more you know, the faster your money will grow. Knowledge really is power when it comes to investing. Reading this book is an important part of the research stage but you should also ensure you conduct plenty of specific research about the investments you have chosen.

Research can come in many forms and might involve reading the personal finance pages of the weekend press, listening to investment experts or meeting with your investment adviser. The golden rule here is only to make an investment you understand. Too many investments end in disappointment because not enough time was taken, before the investment was made, to truly understand what was involved.

Plan

Make a plan and then stick to it. Planning your investments means linking your objectives very closely to your investment choices. You need to have a very clear reason for investing money. This might be as simple as getting a better return than cash but could be connected with life goals, such as becoming debt free or sending your children to a private school.

Brilliant investment plans should always have a SMART measurement. This means they should be:

- **S**pecific,
- **M**easurable,
- **A**chievable,
- **R**ealistic and
- **T**ime sensitive.

An investment plan that fails to meet these criteria is likely to lead to mediocre returns or unexpected losses.

Review

Making an investment and leaving it alone for ten years is rarely a good idea. A brilliant investment plan is reviewed on at least an annual basis and sometimes more frequently. This review should involve more research, to ensure that the facts about the investment remain the same, along with revisions to your investment plan, if required.

> circumstances and objectives change

Circumstances and objectives change. It is wrong to assume that your objectives today will continue to be the same in several years' time. When I speak to disappointed investors they have often failed to meet their goals simply because the goal posts have moved. A little action when it is early enough to make a difference can make all the difference between a poor and a brilliant investment.

When things go (badly) wrong

History gives us some fantastic (but quite scary) examples of investments going badly wrong. Here are some cautionary tales from history which should help you to spot the signs of a poor investment opportunity or an overheated investment market.

brilliant example

The Wall Street Crash

Back in 1929 the USA experienced one of the worst stock market crashes in recorded history. There was a five-year long 'bull market', when prices increased by a multiple of five, which finished on 24 October 1929.

The bull market came to an end on a day known in history as 'Black Thursday'. Share prices continued to fall for a month after this initial crash. It took until the mid-1950s before stock prices on Wall Street returned to their pre-1929 level.

brilliant definition

A 'bull market' is a period of increasing investment returns, usually fuelled by greater confidence from investors who believe that investments will keep going up and up.

To put this in perspective, investors who had invested just before the Wall Street Crash would have needed to wait over 20 years before they got their money back. This assumes that they did not just panic and sell their investments when the crash started. Most investors did and lost everything.

In the run up to the Wall Street Crash a large number of people had been paying over the odds for investments. In some cases they had even been borrowing money to buy shares – a very high-risk strategy. The crash was made worse by panic selling and other stock markets introduced systems to prevent this sort of panic selling occurring in the future.

> the crash was made worse by panic selling

▶ brilliant example

The Dot Com Bubble

This took place between 1995 and 2001 when stock markets witnessed massive growth as a result of investment in internet sector companies. These companies are often called 'dot coms'. The concept of an internet business was relatively new at the time and investors were piling money into previously untested business models.

◆ brilliant definition

An 'investment bubble' occurs when investors buy investments based on past performance and the general expectation that they will continue to do well. This means that the company investors are investing in is not necessarily worth the money they are paying for it. The bubble builds and often 'bursts' when the real value of the investment is recognised.

Here are some final brilliant examples.

▶ brilliant examples

The South Sea Bubble

A much older example of an investment bubble took place in the early 18th century. Speculation in the shares of The South Sea Company was followed by a share price crash in September 1720. The company had exclusive trading rights in Spanish South America.

Investors were piling money into this company as a result of the rumours the company released about the prospects for share price growth. The company even gave free shares to politicians before revealing the names of these high-profile investors.

As a result of these very shady activities, the share price rose from £128 in January 1720 to £550 in May of that year. Eventually the share price went up to over £1,000 in early August 1720. Before the end of the year the price had crashed back to £100.

Black Wednesday

On 16 September 1992 the pound sterling was removed from the European Exchange Rate Mechanism as a result of the activity of currency speculators. One currency speculator, George Soros, made over US$1 billion as a result of this currency speculation. Currency speculation like this worked by investors buying foreign currency with the intention of buying back pounds when they had fallen in value, thereby making a profit.

Black Wednesday was later calculated to have cost the UK Government around £3.4 billion. At the time, interest rates stood at 12% to encourage currency investors to buy pounds rather than foreign currency.

The Enron Scandal

Enron was a US energy company based in Texas. In 2001 it filed for bankruptcy and then various forms of accountancy fraud were revealed which had previously propped up the financial viability of the company. When this scandal was made public the share price plummeted from US$90 to 30 cents. A criminal investigation of Enron followed.

Something else to consider before you invest

Investing money successfully is more about being in the right type of investment at the right time. Choosing the best company shares or investment funds can add some value, but it is your exposure to the broad investment type that makes most of the difference between success and failure.

Within my own firm of investment advisers we put a lot of emphasis on 'asset allocation'. The selection of individual

> we put a lot of emphasis on 'asset allocation'

shares or funds is still important, but once you see how a monkey can do this as well as an investment expert, you will also put a lot of emphasis on asset allocation.

brilliant definition

Asset allocation describes how much of your investments are invested in each of the main investment types (also known as asset classes). We cover these in more detail in the next chapter, but they are cash, fixed interest securities, company shares and property.

To prove that stock picking does not necessarily add value, we need only look to America where a website charts the progress of a monkey, called Leonard, against a television investment pundit. Leonard is just an average monkey but has the nickname 'Leonard the wonder monkey' because of his aptitude for selecting investments. Every time the investment expert makes his investment recommendations the monkey gets to choose stocks, at random, from the same selection. After 30 days they see who picked the best stocks.

As things stand when I write this, the TV expert picked winning stocks 49.33% of the time. The monkey managed to pick winning stocks 50.01% of the time! The average return on investment – calculated by dividing the returns for each selection by the number of selections – was 0.24% for the expert and 0.43% for the monkey. Leonard is often the winner in this little investment competition between man and monkey.

> Leonard is often the winner in this little investment competition

This just goes to show you that picking stocks at random can be just as effective as taking professional advice from an investment expert. Either that or the people behind this particular website have managed to find themselves a very talented monkey. I doubt the latter reason.

Summary

● It is important to understand how compounding, pound cost averaging and the time value of money could affect your investments. They sound slightly technical but are actually very simple concepts. Once you have managed to get your head around these concepts the rest will follow easily.

● If you know what basic investment mistakes look like, you will be able to avoid them. My top five basic investment mistakes include chasing past performance, short-term investing and putting all of your eggs in one basket. Learn about these mistakes so you do not make them.

● There are three things to consider and do every time you invest your money – research, plan and review. By following these three steps each and every time you make an investment you will always be on track to make a brilliant investment.

● History is full of examples of investments going badly wrong. By getting to know some of these examples you will know what signs to look for and, hopefully, be able to avoid them in the future.

● Asset allocation is much more important than picking funds or company shares. Being in the right investment type is the most important lesson for the brilliant investor. Picking winning funds or shares is a mug's game – even a monkey will tell you that!

CHAPTER 3

Risk and
reward

Understanding risk and reward is essential for the brilliant investor. Risk and reward are fundamental investment concepts. There is a clear link between the two. When you take more risk you stand the chance of getting a greater reward. Less risk means less potential for reward. Likewise, if you want a higher reward you need to take more risk. Both risk and reward are clearly linked and if you have one you cannot escape the other.

Once you have read this chapter you will have an excellent understanding of this very special relationship between risk and reward. We will look at the different types of risk (yes, there is more than one type!), how the up and down motion of investments can affect your decisions, the easy way to decide how much risk you feel comfortable taking and then the science bit. Don't worry about the science bit: it's the sort of science that once you know it will make you say 'ahhhh'. Science like that is always good!

What does 'risk' mean?

Just what does risk mean in an investment context? The most common type of investment risk is capital risk. This is simply the risk that the value of your money will fall. This type of investment risk is pretty easy to understand and describe. One day your money is worth £1,000 and there is a risk that the next day it will fall to £800. Capital risk is at the forefront of the investor's mind because it is easy to quantify. It is the type of risk that most of us like to avoid because it is never nice to see our money drop in value.

However, capital risk is not the only type of risk to consider when you are on the path to becoming a brilliant investor. If you only think about capital risk you are probably going to miss out on the bigger picture. I hate to be the one to tell you this, but capital risk is the least of your worries!

> capital risk is the least of your worries

Risk comes in different shapes and sizes

Focusing on capital risk ignores the potential perils of the other main types of investment risk:

- currency risk
- liquidity risk
- income risk
- interest rate risk
- financial risk

Here is a brief explanation of each one. Do not look at capital risk in isolation without first of all deciding if any of these other types of risk might screw up your investments. They may not always apply to the investment you are considering, but where they do apply their impact can be just as devastating as capital risk.

When the exchange rate changes

If you invest in US dollars (or euros, Japanese yen or Chinese renminbi) then you are exposed to 'currency risk'. This is what happens when you invest in a currency other than the one you use at home (so, pounds sterling for most readers of this book).

Currency risk is the risk of the currency in which you are investing going down in value before you convert the money back into your own currency. In some cases this can represent a significant risk. Smaller economies, in particular, tend to have more volatile currencies, which can lead to a greater loss in value than capital risk. There is greater currency risk associated with an investment in Cambodian riels than an investment in US dollars.

Currency risk is one reason why UK investors often keep a large part of their investment portfolio in UK investments. Introducing currency risk to a normally cautious portfolio can substantially increase the overall risk level. However, with greater risk comes the prospect for greater rewards. Currency risk can work both ways!

> currency risk can work both ways

When you can't sell the investment

When you have trouble selling an investment and realising it for cash, you are experiencing liquidity risk. At one extreme this type of risk means that nobody is interested in buying your investment. More typically it means that the market for an investment is quite limited and this suppresses the price you can get. The outcome is usually the same – you either get lumped with an investment you no longer want or you have to offload it for a much cheaper price.

Think of liquidity risk as like trying to sell a car when there are only a couple of potential buyers (and lots of other people trying to sell the same type of car!). You are unlikely to get a very good price because there is plenty of choice for the buyer so they can choose to buy the cheapest vehicle.

Liquidity risk is quite common, particularly in more specialist investment markets. You will even find liquidity risk within some mainstream property funds. This is because getting your cash out of the property fund sometimes means the manager has to flog a particular property to raise the cash to give you. Many property funds therefore contain rules preventing instant access to your cash if there is not enough cash in the bank to pay you without first selling a property. Harsh but fair.

When the income level falls

Income risk is the chance that your chosen investment will fail to provide you with the level of income you need. Depending on your other sources of income, a drop in the level of income generated by your investments can be worse than a drop in the capital value.

> this type of risk is particularly relevant for older investors

This type of risk is particularly relevant for older investors who might be investing their capital to generate an income in retirement. If the income from the investment does not meet your requirements then this particular type of risk might be more serious than capital risk. In fact, the impact of income risk can often lead to a need to erode your capital. The long-term effect of eating into your capital is to reduce the income return yet further, or at least create the need to expose your money to even greater risk to get the same level of income as before.

When interest rates go sky high

Interest rate changes can be a positive or a negative thing. If you are a saver then a rise in interest rates is usually viewed favourably. The interest you get on your bank or building society account will go up, hopefully in line with the interest rate rise.

If you are a borrower (with a mortgage, store cards, personal loans, etc.) then an increase in interest rates is less favourable. It means that the cost of your borrowing goes up and you are left with less disposable income as a result.

Interest rate risk is, therefore, relevant for both investors and borrowers.

When there are 'dodgy dealings' within the company

Any disruption to the internal workings of an investment can be classed as financial risk. The best example of financial risk in recent years is the scandal that engulfed Enron Corporation, an energy company in the USA. After revealing a major case of internal accounting fraud it filed for bankruptcy in 2001. This meant financial loss for those investors and funds that had invested their money in Enron.

brilliant tip

An effective way to avoid the perils of financial risk is to spread your investment around.

Keeping all of your eggs in one basket is a great way to lose all of your money if things go wrong. Diversification is the key to avoiding financial risk.

The up and down movement of investments

As advisers we are always keen to point out a third dimension to the risk and reward relationship – volatility. Increased risk typically means more volatility as well. Volatility is best explained as the up and down movement in value of a particular investment. It is a bit like a boat sailing on ocean waves.

An investment with greater volatility means more risk because there is a greater chance it will be at a lower value when you decide to sell the investment. Highly volatile investments are a particularly bad idea for people who are close to the time when they need to get their hands on the cash.

brilliant tip

If you are getting closer to retirement it usually makes sense to move your pension funds into less volatile investments so you are not at the mercy of short-term price fluctuations. A loss of 20% of your pension fund the week before retirement is far more serious than if it happens ten years earlier!

Volatility does not actually matter very much when you are investing your money, unless . . .

- It is close to a time when you need to sell your investments, like the day you want to retire.
- Your emotions drive you to sell your investments if you see them plummet in value.
- You are the sort of short-term investor who checks the value of your portfolio on a daily basis (or even more frequently!).

> volatility can be a very positive thing

In fact, volatility can be a very positive thing. A more volatile investment creates more frequent buying opportunities. If you know the market is rising and falling in value you might be able to spot a time when you can invest in a cheaper market. People who invest their money on a regular basis (for example, monthly) benefit from more volatile markets as a result of something called 'pound cost averaging' (see the previous chapter).

Volatility is measured by the 'standard deviation' of its rate of return. This is a technical term but best described as how far away from the average rate of return your investment is likely to move in any single year. The greater the standard deviation of an investment, the more volatile it will be.

You don't need to worry about the term 'standard deviation' but it is useful to know what it means just in case an investment adviser drops it into a conversation to try to look clever!

How much risk should I take?

When you employ the services of a professional investment adviser they will spend a great deal of time talking about risk. Or at least they should! Your attitude towards investment risk is a key factor in any advice they give you about how to invest your money. Any adviser worth

> your attitude towards investment risk is a key factor

their salt will spend a lot of time talking to you about your attitude towards risk to try to tease out important information.

It is not sufficient for them to try to broadly categorise you simply as a 'cautious', 'balanced' or 'adventurous' investor. If this is the rapid outcome of a short discussion about how much risk you feel comfortable taking you should pack up and leave their office.

Many investment advisers are now starting to use sophisticated risk profiling tools as part of their risk analysis process. These often make use of psychometric questions and other tools from the world of psychology to try to build up a more accurate picture of your attitude towards risk. Even with these sophisticated tools the adviser should still spend time talking to you about your personal view of investment risk and then ensure any recommendations closely match this profile.

> **brilliant** tip
>
> Spend time talking to your adviser about risk and don't let them pigeon-hole you into a broad risk category.

Your risk profile can often lead to a conflict with your investment objectives as these may not be achievable within the budget you have allocated and the level of risk you are prepared to take. For this reason it might be necessary to alter your objectives once you have established the risk profile you feel most comfortable with.

Risk has an awful lot to do with comfort. Before you make any investment you need to consider how comfortable you would feel if it dropped in value either more frequently or to a greater degree than you wanted. The great thing about investment is that everyone has choice about how much risk they want to take with their money. You can feel as comfortable as you like as a brilliant investor.

Five key drivers of risk

It is possible to work out your own risk profile without the hassle (and expense) of a professional investment adviser. In order to do this you should think carefully about the following five factors:

1 **Knowledge** – the more knowledgeable you are about investments, the more risk you are likely to be able to take. Knowledge is power when it comes to being a brilliant investor.

2 **Experience** – experienced investors tend to take more risk than inexperienced investors. This is because they have 'been there' before and know how it felt to take risks with their money. You can always change your risk profile over time. It is far better to start off taking less risk and gradually increase this over time as you get more confident.

3 **Reactions** – how would you react if your investment fell in value overnight? There are three ways investors tend to react to this happening to them: they sell what is left, do nothing or buy more investments. If you would sell your investments you are likely to be risk averse. Those investors who plan to buy more when their investments drop in value have a greater appetite for risk.

4 **Feelings** – think about how you normally feel after making a significant financial decision. Personally I often feel quite bad when I spend a lot of money or make a big investment. It is a form of buyer's remorse. Not everyone gets this and those who feel fine after big financial deals usually have a higher risk profile.

5 **Greed** – this often drives your attitude to risk. If you want bigger returns then you will accept you have to take more risk to get them. If you are satisfied with more modest investment returns you probably have a more modest attitude to risk.

Any risk profiling exercise should consider at least these five factors. It is the combination of your attitudes towards each of these five that makes up your overall attitude towards investment risk. Whilst you might be a high-risk investor in respect of one of these factors, the others can drag your risk profile down to a more realistic level.

brilliant tip

Remember – if in doubt, start with lower-risk investments and work your way up the risk spectrum gradually. You will feel better about taking more risk over time than getting your fingers burnt with higher-risk investments straight away.

Watch out for 'risky shift'

It is always best to make decisions about investment risk on your own. Making decisions in a group of people can lead to a strange phenomenon known as 'risky shift'.

> make decisions about investment risk on your own

'Risky shift' is the tendency for decisions made in a group to result in a more adventurous view of risk. Because we assume that other members of a group will be prepared to take more risk than we normally would we tend to adjust our risk profile to meet our expectations. This leads to 'risky shift'.

It is, of course, unlikely that you would ever make your brilliant investment decisions in a big group. However, if you ever find yourself in a large group of people agreeing to bungee jump you might want to stop and consider if some 'risky shift' has just taken place!

Risk profiles can change

It's not unusual for an investor to have several different investment risk profiles. Your risk profile is likely to vary depending on the investment objective under consideration. One of the biggest mistakes made by novice investors is to try to match a single risk profile to each one of their various risk profiles.

For example, an investor might have a different view of risk when thinking about repaying their mortgage in comparison to their risk profile for retirement planning. It is quite common for an investor to have a cautious attitude to risk for paying off the mortgage but a more speculative risk profile for longer-term retirement planning.

brilliant tip

There is nothing wrong with having a different risk profile for different financial objectives.

Don't be afraid to articulate a different risk profile for different objectives. If your investment adviser attempts to pigeon-hole you into a single risk profile for every single investment objective you might take this as a sign that you should be looking for a new adviser.

Risk profiles also change as a result of time and experience. We very often find that our clients want to revise their risk profiles after a couple of years of exposure to a more cautious risk profile. Our experiences of investment volatility and performance often shape the way we think about risk and reward.

If you are planning a change to your risk profile my advice is to take things slowly. Moving from a very cautious risk profile to a very speculative risk profile is not a good move to make overnight. Consider moving away from your cautious risk profile in gradual stages, leaving plenty of time between each move to see how you feel about it. Remember that you can move down the risk spectrum as well as up.

> you can move down the risk spectrum as well as up

The theory behind investment risk

To understand risk in the context of your investment decisions you need to know about *modern portfolio theory*. This explains how investing in lots of different things (diversification) can be used to build a brilliant investment portfolio.

The starting point for this theory is that investors want to avoid unnecessary risk. Given the choice of two different investment options with the same likely returns, most investors would choose the one that was the least risky. This sounds fairly reasonable if you think about it. Brilliant investors only take greater levels of risk in return for the potential for greater investment returns. This is a basic building block of the relationship between investment risk and reward. There is no sense in risking your money unless you are going to get rewarded for taking that risk.

Within a brilliant investment portfolio it is possible to reduce risk through greater diversification. This means investing in different investments that are likely to behave differently. By increasing diversification it is often possible to build an investment portfolio with the same potential for returns but lower overall levels of risk. When you add another investment to an existing portfolio it can reduce the overall level of risk if it is negatively correlated to the existing investments. That is to say, if the new investment will behave in a different way to the existing investments.

The efficient frontier

Now that you understand the building blocks behind modern portfolio theory you can move on to the next level. The graphical application of modern portfolio theory comes in the form of the *efficient frontier*. This is a line showing the most efficient investment return for a given level of risk. It shows that to get the potential for greater reward you need to take more risk.

> think of the efficient frontier as a glass ceiling

Think of the efficient frontier as a glass ceiling. If you want to get a better investment return it will always involve taking more risk, assuming that your portfolio already sits on the line drawn by the efficient frontier. In my experience most investment portfolios are nowhere near the efficient frontier line. This means that they are taking more risk than they need to be for the returns they are likely to gain. It's a shame that this is the case because nobody likes taking more risk than they need to.

When we plot portfolios on the efficient frontier for our clients they appreciate how by tweaking the contents of their portfolio they can get better potential investment returns and maintain exactly the same level of risk. Alternatively, they can reduce the level of risk within their portfolio but keep the same potential for returns as they have within their inefficient portfolio.

It's science, but it's very practical investment science!

Summary

- 'Capital risk' is important, but remember to consider the other main types of investment risk – currency, liquidity, income, interest rate and financial risk. Investment risk comes in many different shapes and sizes. Watch out for it!

- Volatility adds a third dimension to the relationship between risk and reward. Greater volatility can help investors who invest their money on a regular basis, as a result of pound cost averaging. Volatility is best avoided if you are close to the time when you need your money.

- To assess your own attitude towards investment risk you need to think long and hard about five factors – your knowledge, experience, reactions, feelings and greed.

- Risk profiles can change over time and can be different for different investment objectives. Never allow an investment adviser to pigeon-hole you into a single risk profile for all of your objectives.

- Modern portfolio theory is essential to understand if you want to become a brilliant investor. Always think about risk at the level of your whole investment portfolio and not at the level of individual investments.

CHAPTER 4

Places to invest your money

Once you understand the basics of being a brilliant investor and have managed to get a good handle on your attitude towards investment risk, reward and volatility, you need to know where to invest your money.

This chapter looks at each of the four main types of investment – cash, fixed interest securities, property and equities (company shares). These four asset classes form the basis of every investment decision you will ever make.

This chapter also explains some of the actual investment options within each asset class you might come across when making your investment decisions.

Too much choice!

There are simply too many investment options to choose from! One of the reasons why people are often put off investing their hard-earned cash is that there are so many choices and options that they end up confused by the complexity.

The purpose of this chapter is to describe the different places where you might invest your money and the advantages and disadvantages of each of those choices. I am going to take you step by step through this and by the time you have finished reading this chapter you should have a much better understanding of what you might actually do with your money to become a brilliant investor.

Asset classes

A good starting point might be to consider what are known as investment asset classes.

investment asset classes are the investment 'engine'

Investment asset classes are, broadly speaking, the investment 'engine' of any investment that you choose. Whatever investment you buy it will contain one or more of these investment asset classes. Each of them has different characteristics and also different degrees of investment risk, reward and volatility.

An asset class is the broad type of investment. Your house, for example, sits within the property asset class. Company shares would fall into the equity asset class. An asset class is the building block of an investment portfolio. By understanding the main features of each asset class you will be able to build a solid foundation for your brilliant investments.

Different investment experts will claim there are different numbers of investment asset classes but for the sake of simplicity, but without losing any accuracy, I will start with the main four. I will also describe variations of these within the general theme.

The main four investment asset classes are:

● cash
● fixed interest
● property and
● equities.

I am going to describe them in what I believe is an ascending order of investment risk, starting with cash.

Cash is king

The first main investment asset class to look at is cash.

We all know that cash is the coins and notes in our purses, wallets and pockets (and down the back of the sofa!). In the context of investment though I mean money that we have in bank, building society or National Savings & Investment accounts. We deposit our money with these institutions and effectively we are lending our money to them. In return they reward us by adding interest to our accounts.

There is a multitude of accounts to choose from. These accounts form the products that I mentioned earlier and I will explain more about them later.

Important features of cash

Cash has certain important features that the brilliant investor needs to consider.

It is generally considered to be the safest of the investment asset classes from a risk perspective. We usually refer to cash as 'savings' rather than investments.

If I place £100 in a deposit account with my bank this afternoon and I go back to take it out at the end of the month or year I expect to get at least my £100 back. If I wait ten years before I take my money out I again expect to get at least £100.

Of course I would be disappointed if I got only £100 back! I would expect to get my £100 plus some interest. Interest is the reward we receive for keeping our cash on deposit with a bank or building society. They are happy to reward us by paying interest because they can use our cash to invest and make more money.

> interest is the reward we receive for keeping our cash on deposit

I will of course not get any capital growth on my £100 original capital as it is still £100. Anything else on top is interest, or indeed interest earned on interest. Interest is a type of investment income rather than growth. This income is usually added to your savings rather than paid out to you, although some savings accounts will pay you the interest on a monthly or annual basis if you ask nicely.

Cashing in on the risks

So the most positive virtue of cash as an investment asset class is that you have a degree of security. But cash is not without risk. As discussed earlier in this book, investment risk is about more than just the risk of capital loss.

There are three risks you need to consider when thinking about investing in cash.

Inflation risk

The first risk to consider is *inflation risk*.

Money that is kept as cash for a very long time may actually lose value. This is not because you get less than your £100 back but because price inflation in the long term tends to erode the buying power of your money.

The simple fact of the matter is that £100 today will not buy you £100 worth of goods in ten years' time. In fact, if price inflation ran at a rather modest 4% a year, the cost of buying £100 worth of goods in ten years' time would be around £148. We do not tend to notice inflation over the shorter term, but it should be a concern if you want to keep your money in cash for the longer term. Price inflation is a very good reason to avoid keeping all of your money in cash for the long term.

To beat inflation risk you need to find a savings account that, after tax has been deducted, will pay you a higher rate of interest than the rate of price inflation. This is nearly impossible over the long term. Therefore it is rather inevitable that your cash will lose value over time.

Institutional risk

The second risk to think about is *institutional risk.*

By this I mean that you may lose your capital if the institution that you deposit your money with goes bust and it has fewer assets than liabilities. Now I accept that if your money is with a UK institution this is a little unlikely, although not impossible. The old adage about 'not keeping all your eggs in one basket' is not a bad one to follow here – spread your savings around and sleep much more comfortably at night!

> spread your savings around and sleep much more comfortably at night!

Banks and building societies in the UK are covered by a safety net scheme known as the Financial Services Compensation Scheme (FSCS). This means that if they go out of business and cannot afford to repay savers, the scheme will offer some compensation.

It is by no means a way of recovering all of your money. For deposits the maximum is limited to £31,700 per person. In practical terms £2,000 is recoverable at a rate of 100% and the next £33,000 at 90%. This level of compensation is usually sufficient for a typical saver but if you are putting bigger sums in a bank or building society account you need to be aware of the limitations of this compensation scheme.

Lost opportunity risk

The third risk to consider with cash is known as *lost opportunity risk.*

This is the risk of missing out on better investment returns elsewhere because your money is in safe, predictable cash.

Let's say that I keep my cash on deposit and earn 5% interest. However, I could have invested that cash in the stock market and earned 15% growth. I might feel that the cash whilst less 'risky' has caused me to miss out on 10% extra return.

Many investors stick to cash when they feel the market will underperform in the short term but end up losing out on bigger returns as a result. It is all too easy to 'miss the boat' if your investments are in cash and the investment markets start to rise.

If staying in cash offers you some comfort then this is no bad thing, but you need to be prepared for the risk that your returns from cash will be dismal in comparison with the returns from other investment opportunities.

Getting the best returns

If you decide to stick with cash for part of your brilliant investment portfolio then you need to get the best possible returns. Banks and building societies are all too happy to let investors leave their money in accounts paying dismal rates of interest. Low interest rates mean bigger profits for the banks and building societies.

brilliant tip

You can often get a more competitive rate of interest if you are prepared to give some notice before withdrawing your cash. Select a 30- or 90-day notice account to get the highest rates of return on your cash.

To get the best interest rates you need to shop around. The weekend papers are full of best buy tables that will show you how much interest you can get for the amount of cash you have.

Once you have found a competitive rate you need to review it on a regular basis. At least once a year compare your interest rate to the rest of the market. Banks love lazy customers who do not bother moving their money once interest rates start to fall. Be prepared to be a 'rate tart' and move your money around to get the best interest rate.

be prepared to be a 'rate tart'

brilliant tip

Watch out for special introductory offers that come to an abrupt end after a short period of time. These offers make the headline interest rate look really competitive but don't tend to last for long.

Fixed interest securities

After cash, the next main investment asset class is called fixed interest securities.

Put simply, fixed interest securities are a way of borrowing money by governments, local authorities or businesses.

When any of these institutions want to borrow some money they may issue what are known as 'bonds'. We then lend them our money in return for which they will promise two things:

- Firstly they will pay us a fixed rate of interest (hence the name of this asset class).
- Secondly they will, at some point in the future, return to us the money that we lent them.

It is a reasonable deal and the sort of arrangement you would expect whenever someone borrowed money from you.

The rate of interest is agreed in advance and fixed at the outset. The term of the borrowing is also usually fixed at the outset. Sometimes this is open ended as there is no fixed date for repayment of the loan. If this seems more complicated than simply depositing your money in a cash account with a bank, building society or National Savings & Investments, do not worry, as all will be explained!

Two good reasons for investing in bonds

There are two very good reasons why you might consider investing in fixed interest securities.

The first is (and excuse me for the obvious statement here) the interest rate is fixed. If you deposit your money with a bank the interest rate is usually variable as the rate can go up and down in the future. The income from fixed interest securities might typically be paid to you every six months.

> there may be some prospect of capital growth in the future

The second difference is that with fixed interest securities there may be some prospect of capital growth in the future. You will remember that with cash there is no capital growth? With fixed interest securities there may well be a market for these bonds. In other words individuals and institutions may want to buy and sell them.

Where there is a market then the economic laws of supply and demand will apply. Depending upon this and other economic conditions the price paid for bonds may vary.

Of course with capital growth comes the prospect of capital loss and therefore the value can go down as well as up. Fixed interest securities are therefore not without risk. While the interest rate applied to these investments is fixed, the capital value can fluctuate which means the actual income paid can go up and down.

Some investors assume that because the interest is fixed so is the value of their investment.

Let us take a look at two very distinct types of fixed interest securities – gilts and corporate bonds.

Gilt-edged securities

These represent government borrowing and are considered to be the most secure form of fixed interest security investment. The repayment of the invested money and the interest due are both guaranteed by the Government.

From a tax perspective, gilts are free from capital gains tax but the interest is paid gross and is subject to income tax.

> gilts are free from capital gains tax

Most gilts provide a fixed rate of interest through to their maturity (known as a redemption date). There are various redemption dates grouped into:

- 'shorts' (less than five years to redemption),
- 'medium' (between five and 15 years to redemption),
- 'long' (over 15 years to redemption) and
- 'undated' (which have no specific redemption date).

brilliant definition

The name 'gilt-edged' comes from the traditional practice of printing these investment certificates on paper with gold, or 'gilt', edges.

Corporate bonds

These represent borrowing by companies. They are, therefore, less secure than gilts because of course they are not backed by the Government. Unlike the UK Government, companies can go bust and investors might lose all their money – both the capital they are owed and any interest due.

Fixed interest rates for corporate bonds tend to be higher than gilts because of the extra risk that the investor takes. This is known as a *risk premium*. The interest rate becomes higher depending on the financial security of the company issuing the bonds. The security of these companies is often rated by independent ratings companies which 'score' the company according to how risky it is.

If a company represents a higher risk because it is financially unstable you would expect to get a better rate of return. You are, after all, taking more risk by lending it money.

Profiting from property

The third main asset class to consider is property.

Property has been one of the most popular investments over the past decade. Investors have had a love affair with property for a number of reasons. There are two main rewards for investing in property.

The first reward is the potential for capital growth. If you buy a property tomorrow you hope to be able to sell it in ten years' time for a significantly higher price. Anyone who owns their own house (or keeps an eye on residential property prices) will know that this has certainly been true in recent years. The rate at which property prices have increased each year (known as property price inflation) has been far higher than average. This level of growth often leads commentators to predict a price crash on the basis that 'what goes up must come down'.

Whilst property prices can go down as well as up, you would typically expect them to increase over the longer term.

The second reward for investing in property is rental income. During the time you own a property you would expect the person who lives or works there (the tenant) to pay you a rent. This rental income is often used by the brilliant property investor to cover the costs of investing in property.

What costs? Well, property investors tend to borrow money to invest with. They then use the rental income to pay the interest on this borrowed money. The reason for doing this is the expectation of long-term growth in the value of the property. Someone else is effectively financing your investments.

> someone else is effectively financing your investments

In the context of brilliant investing, there are three different types of property to know about:

- residential,
- commercial and
- property company shares.

The property you live in

Most people are familiar with residential property. This segment of the property asset class covers the places people live. From an investment perspective it normally excludes your own home. That is not to say that your home has no value within your personal financial planning.

Our homes are often our largest assets. They are not, however, strictly investments because we cannot sell them and realise the cash. We all need a place to live! Our homes also fail to provide a steady stream of income. Remember that investment property comes with two rewards – capital growth and income.

The brilliant investor is normally more interested in 'buy-to-let' property. This is the sort of property that you 'buy' with the intention of 'letting' (or renting) to a tenant in return for rental income. A feature of property investment is that you can borrow money, in the form of a mortgage, to make the investment and buy the property. The rental income is then used to pay the interest charges on the mortgage.

Buy-to-let investment could fill an entire book. It has become an extremely popular investment option for people who want to invest in something they can look at and touch. We get a sense of certainty from investing in a tangible asset like property.

This sort of property investment comes with risks. The biggest risks to consider surround the prospect for capital growth, loss of income and the inability to pay the cost of borrowing.

Take a minute to think through the worst case scenario.

Imagine that you invest in a property for £100,000. You have managed to raise a mortgage for £85,000 which is usually the most you can borrow, as a percentage, with a buy-to-let mortgage. One year into your brilliant property investment things start to go wrong. The property market crashes, your tenant stops paying rent and the interest rate on your mortgage skyrockets. You can no longer afford to pay the mortgage and are forced into selling the property for less than you paid for it.

This might well be the worst case scenario but it is not completely impossible. As with any investment you should go into it with your eyes wide open. Think about the risk and work out how you can manage it. If the risks described above seem reasonable and you can handle the thought of taking on more debt, then property investing might just be a good option for you to consider.

brilliant tip

Be warned!

As a parting thought on residential property investing, be warned that the people who run weekend 'get rich quick from property' type seminars are probably not too keen to point out these risks. They prefer to make you think that property investment is highly complex with lots of 'secrets' that they can sell to you. The reality is that you can stick to the lessons from this book and make a brilliant property investment. It is just another investment asset class. All of the normal rules of brilliant investing apply.

The property you work in

Commercial property includes shops, offices, warehouses and factories, and the like. Most of these are made of bricks and mortar just like our homes. The main difference is the tenants. Unlike residential property, it will be those working in these properties who pay the rent, typically businesses.

Investing in commercial property is very similar to investing in residential property but there are a few important differences.

- Firstly, the prices tend to be higher. A large office block is bound to cost more than a three-bedroom house.

- Secondly, it is often the case that tenants agree to stay for much longer. Commercial property contracts are commonly for ten or 15 years. Compare this to a six-month residential property rental agreement and you will see that commercial property can provide a much more predictable stream of income.

The commercial property market tends to be a bit more stable than residential property. It rarely sees the same spectacular capital growth seen in flats and houses. As a result of this it can often avoid big price falls as well. This makes commercial property a more attractive investment option for investors at the more cautious end of the risk spectrum.

Property company shares

A final property investment option is not traditional bricks and mortar at all, but instead shares in companies that, in turn, invest in property or land. This is known as 'indirect' property investment, as you are not investing directly in real property but getting an indirect benefit from a company that does invest in these properties.

The main benefit of investing in property in this way is easy access to your money. To get your cash back from a direct property investment you need to sell the property. This can be time consuming and expensive, assuming that you can actually find someone who is prepared to pay the price you are after. Selling property company shares is fast and relatively cheap.

> selling property company shares is fast and relatively cheap

Property companies tend to invest in a wide range of individual properties and this should have a risk reducing effect. It is easier to get exposure to 20 properties by investing in company shares than it is for an individual investor to do this directly.

The main drawback of investing in property in this way is volatility. You are investing in company shares rather than bricks and mortar. Share prices can fluctuate in value a lot more than direct property investment. The value of your shares will be based on both the value of the properties the company invests in and investor demand for the shares. This additional factor increases the risk associated with investing in property company shares.

Just because you are buying company shares rather than real property, the costs of buying the property are still there for investors to pay. They might be harder to spot but property investment is expensive and this expense will have an impact on investment returns.

Shares in a company

The fourth main asset class, and probably the main one people think of from an investment perspective, is called *equities*.

Equities are more commonly known as company shares. By company shares we mean that the investor has a 'share' in the ownership and profits of a business.

There are many different kinds of company shares but the ones we are considering here are known as *ordinary shares*, although I would argue that there is very little that is ordinary about them.

As with property there are two potential rewards for the brilliant investor who buys and sells company shares. The first is that you have a share of the company profits. A share in the profits of a business is known as a *dividend*. Dividends can be paid to the investor when the company whose shares we own makes a profit. It is also possible that these dividend payments can increase over time and therefore produce a rising level of income for the investor.

> dividend payments can increase over time

The second reward for company share owners is that hopefully the price that you pay for your shares today is lower than the price that you get when you sell them in the future.

There are a large number of factors that will determine whether we do get a higher (or lower) price for our shares when we come to sell them. How well the company performs and what people think of its prospects are probably the two most important factors.

Here we are talking about what are known as *quoted shares*, which means their prices are quoted on a stock market. The most important market for the UK investor is the London Stock Exchange (LSE). Within that stock market the FTSE 100 is one 'index' that measures the performance of the top 100 listed company shares.

investing in shares is not without risk

Investing in shares is not without risk. The next time you listen to the TV or radio news and hear that the FTSE 100 has fallen 175 points and wiped £3 billion off the value of company shares consider that this means that investors have seen the value of their portfolios fall.

There may be prolonged periods where share prices seem to do nothing but fall in value but of course there are also periods where the opposite happens and real and valuable growth is experienced by investors who have invested in shares.

Dividend payments are also not guaranteed for the investor in ordinary shares – they can go up, down or not be paid at all. At the most extreme, a company in whose shares we invest might fail altogether, in which case we might lose all of the money that we have invested.

So much choice – where do I invest?

Once you have chosen between cash, fixed interest securities, property or equities, you would be forgiven for feeling a bit lost and confused. Within each of these four main asset classes sits a whole range of sub-categories. Property has already been segmented in this chapter between residential, commercial and property company shares. Other asset classes have the same sort of segmentation.

The asset class with the most segmentation, probably because it is the biggest investment asset class, is equities. Investments within this asset class can be segmented by size, industry and/or geographical region. This means that you have a choice between investing in large UK financial services companies or smaller Japanese pharmaceutical companies – and just about anything in between!

As a result, the range of investment choices can be bewildering. Before you decide which one is best for you, you need to know about 'correlation'.

> the range of investment choices can be bewildering

The relationship between different investments

The reason it is so important to understand the attributes of the different asset classes is something called *correlation*. Correlation describes the connection or lack of connection between the different investment asset classes.

If you invest in a range of investment asset classes you might benefit from what is called *negative correlation*. This means that when the price of one of the asset classes is rising or falling, the price of a negatively correlated investment asset class is doing the complete opposite. Put more simply than that, the old adage about not having all your investment eggs in one basket can be extended to not having all your investment in the same investment asset class.

Over time this means that negative correlation in your investment portfolio might result in less volatility.

brilliant example

Having 100% of your investments in company shares when the stock market collapses will result in a significant drop in the value of your portfolio. If you had 50% in company shares, 25% in fixed interest securities and 25% in commercial property then the risk could be significantly reduced.

As a result of this negative correlation between different asset classes you might consider investing in more than one asset class at a time to build your brilliant investment portfolio. In fact, I would strongly urge you to consider investing in multiple asset classes at any given time. Even if you are really sure that a particular asset class is going to perform well, invest in some others as well. By spreading your investments around like this you reduce the chances that you will see the value of your total investment portfolio wiped out overnight.

> consider investing in multiple asset classes at any given time

It's a wrap

To actually gain access to an investment you need to invest either directly or via a tax wrapper. Direct investment is a fairly easy concept to understand. It means you are investing without the benefit of any tax privileges or any other special treatment. Investing through a wrapper requires a bit more of an explanation.

A good example of a tax wrapper is an Individual Savings Account (ISA). We come on to talk about these in greater detail in Chapter 6 when we look at tax, but they are briefly looked at here.

An ISA is not an investment at all. It is really a tax wrapper. The investments contained within an ISA are to a large extent protected against the damaging effects of tax because they are included within this wrapper.

In a similar way, investment products are not investments either, they are tax wrappers. By that I mean what really matters are the underlying investments that these products contain. So, for example, a unit trust (which we talk about later) is a tax wrapper and the real investment is the shares or other assets that are held inside the unit trust.

Building an investment portfolio

What I will do next in this chapter is to describe the different ways in which the brilliant investor might invest his or her money into the investment asset classes that I have already described, through the various product wrappers and products in order to build their investment portfolio.

This section does not aim to tell you if a particular product is the most suitable for you. Each of them is structured quite differently although the underlying objectives of each are pretty similar. The suitability of a particular wrapper or product will depend upon your personal investment goals and objectives as well as your current and future tax position.

Direct or collective?

If I take my £100 and buy shares in Marks and Spencer I have made a *direct investment*. If I take my £100 and invest in a unit trust and the investment manager of that unit trust then invests in Marks and Spencer shares (and others) then I have made an *indirect* or *collective investment*.

Similarly, if I buy a shop and that property is registered in my own name it is a direct investment. But if my pension plan invests in a commercial property fund then that is an *indirect* or *collective investment*. It is known as 'collective' because the investment manager collects together money from various investors and uses these monies to buy a range of direct investments. Collective investments are also known as *mutual funds* – a name they picked up from the

> collective investments are also known as *mutual funds*

USA. You might also hear reference made to 'managed funds', which is also an acceptable term used to describe collectives.

Collective investment tends to spread the investor's money across a wide range of different direct investments and this adds to the reduction of risk by diversification. Diversification tells us that it is less risky to invest in 100 shares of £1 each than one share at £100.

Using a collective investment is a good way of getting access to a wider range of investments. A typical investor may not be able to access 50 different investments with the money they have available to invest. If they could get access to these 50 different investments directly then the cost would probably be prohibitive.

brilliant tip

By using a collective investment the brilliant investor can gain economies of scale and make spreading their money amongst different underlying assets more cost effective.

Collective investments come at a price, so it is important to take a closer look at value when considering this investment option. As well as the costs of dealing in different investments the fund must cover the costs of the fund manager. This fund manager remuneration typically works on the basis of a percentage of funds under management. Some fund managers receive a performance related fee; they get paid more if the fund meets or outperforms expectations. Whilst this can be a good incentive for a fund manager, the reality is it can encourage them to take excessive risks. When investing in a fund with a performance related fee structure you need to ensure there are adequate penalties if the manager fails to perform as expected or takes more risk than agreed.

> some fund managers receive a performance related fee

Open or closed?

There are two main types of collective investment funds to consider – open-ended and closed-ended.

Open-ended

The shares (known as *units*) in this type of collective investment fund are a proportion of the underlying fund of assets in the fund. This means that if the fund invested in assets valued at, say, £100,000 and there were 100,000 units issued, each unit would be valued at £1. This structure means that the value of units always reflects the value of underlying assets within the fund.

Unit trusts and OEICs (open-ended investment companies) both work on this basis. Other funds that are open-ended include ICVCs (investment companies with variable capital) and SICAVs (Société d'investissement à capital variable). These last two types of funds are more common in Europe but are becoming increasingly popular with UK investors.

Closed-ended

Unlike open-ended funds, these funds have a set number of shares. These shares are traded and will trade at either a premium or a discount to the value of underlying assets within the fund. This premium or discount is driven by investor demand for the shares. When demand for shares is high the shares will trade at a premium. When demand for shares is low they will trade at a discount – making them cheaper than the underlying assets within the fund. Investment trusts work on this basis.

Other things to watch out for

If you are thinking about investing in collective investment funds there are a number of other things you need to watch out for.

Some collective investment funds have the power to borrow money to invest alongside the money from investors. This is a practice known as *gearing*. It increases the level of risk associated with the fund but also the potential for return. As long as the returns from the fund exceed the cost of borrowing the money, the rate of growth should be faster than a fund without any gearing.

> many collective investment funds will include a commission for the adviser

Many collective investment funds will include a commission for the adviser who sold them. This is often reflected in the annual management charge for the fund and may be 0.25% or 0.5% per annum. If you buy the fund directly from the fund management company this charge often remains in place and just represents additional profit for them. You should either ensure you are receiving a sufficient level of ongoing advice and service from the adviser who sold you the fund or, if you prefer to cut out the middleman, invest through a discount broker who can reduce or remove this additional cost from your investment.

Another drawback to be aware of is that using a collective investment fund removes the shareholder rights you would have received if you had invested directly. These shareholder rights can vary depending on the company, but can include discounts on their products and, more importantly from an investment perspective, the right to vote on important issues at the annual general meeting (AGM). You get these rights if you buy a share directly but not if you invest through a collective investment fund.

Passive or active?

It takes expertise, skill and a huge amount of resource for a fund manager to consistently create market beating investment returns. This may account for the reasons why so many active fund managers fail to achieve the benchmarks they set for themselves. It has been suggested that as many as two-thirds of fund managers fail to consistently meet their self-imposed targets! The brilliant investor might be paying for access to the expertise of a skilled fund manager but this does not guarantee investment success.

If you are as cynical as I am about the ability of fund managers to consistently outperform the market, there is an alternative to costly actively managed funds.

Passive fund management is where the investment funds contain a sample of, for example, shares that replicate a particular index. The best example is the FTSE 100 (the Financial Times Stock Exchange 100) which is the 100 largest UK-based companies by size. A passive fund manager will hold these companies' shares in proportion to the index. The investor therefore sees their investment rise and fall in line with the FTSE 100 index.

Passive fund management is commonly found within 'tracker' funds. These aim to 'track' the performance of a particular investment market or index. Tracker funds tend to have much lower charges than actively managed collective investment funds. In

> tracker funds tend to have much lower charges

the UK the cost of tracker funds is still higher than those available in the USA but this appears to be changing as these funds become more popular with UK investors.

A tracker fund is never going to outperform an index but you may be more comfortable with this approach rather than trusting a fund manager who more often than not might underperform this index.

brilliant tip

Consider whether you are more comfortable with an active or passive approach to investing.

Unit trusts

Unit trusts are a way of investing in a wide range of shares with relatively modest amounts of money. They are also a way of obtaining professional fund management expertise and selection of the underlying assets in a cost effective way.

For the investor who wants the benefits of professional fund management and does not have the personal expertise to select the shares for their portfolio this is a very easy way to invest money. There are very many different fund managers and funds to choose from and they all have set goals and objectives so the investor should be able to find a particular fund that suits their requirements.

A unit trust fund enables the investor to spread the risk of investment because the fund manager can build a balanced portfolio of shares by the pooling together of various investors' funds. There are many different types of funds ranging from general funds – that cover most types of investment markets – to very specific funds – that concentrate on a particular market or sector.

There are funds that are designed to produce high levels of income (not surprisingly called income funds) and others that are designed to produce capital growth. There are also funds that combine these features, for example balanced funds, which seek to produce both growth and income.

A unit trust will have a fund manager but it will also have a custodian, typically a bank, to make sure that the underlying investments are held securely. As the title suggests, a unit trust is created under a trust instrument and that forms the legal structure that adds a degree of financial protection to the investor.

> a unit trust is created under a trust instrument

Expect to pay charges for the services and expertise delivered by the unit trust manager. Typically there will be some form of initial charge of around 5% of the money that you invest and an annual management charge in the range of 0.5% to 1.5% depending upon the nature of the fund (passive funds tend to be cheaper than actively managed funds).

Remember though that the value of your investments in a unit trust can go down as well as up just like the underlying investments. A unit trust manager can only buy shares with the money he has. Except within strictly controlled limits the manager cannot borrow money. However the unit trust manager can create more units. For this reason unit trusts are said to be 'open-ended'.

Investment trusts

Investment trusts are another way of investing in a portfolio of shares. This portfolio of shares is then managed by professional investment managers.

Despite the fact that they have the word 'trust' in the title investment trusts are not trusts, they are instead publicly quoted companies, and are quoted on the London Stock Exchange. Investment trusts are unusual companies though in the sense that they do not manufacture, service or distribute goods and services of any kind. They simply exist to buy the shares in other companies. For this reason they are a form of collective investment fund.

When you invest in an investment trust you purchase the shares in a quoted company. The future value of the shares that you buy depends upon the usual marketplace laws of demand and supply but also on the skills of the investment trust manager. If the manager has a good record of buying the shares in other companies then the investment trust investor might expect to see the value of their shares grow. If the manager is less skilled then of course the underlying value of the shares may go down.

brilliant tip

Investment trusts have a number of advantages for the brilliant investor, low cost being one of them. They also benefit from a spread of risk because the investment trust holds a range of different shares – very important from a risk management perspective.

The shares purchased by the investment trust might not just be the shares in UK companies but might be from companies around the world. As with unit trusts, there are different investment trusts available with different investment objectives. The disadvantages of course are that the value of shares can go down as well as up and that the investor is heavily reliant upon the investment skills of the manager.

> the investor is heavily reliant upon the investment skills of the manager

Unlike a unit trust the investment trust manager can borrow money to buy more shares. This is known as *gearing* and can have both a positive and negative effect. If the manager borrows money and buys more shares that do really well then the underlying value of the investment trust share might increase quite substantially. If on the other hand borrowed money is used to purchase underperforming shares then the investment trust shares might go down in value even more quickly.

Investment trust managers cannot create more shares for potential purchasers and therefore investment trusts are said to be 'closed-ended'.

Open-ended investment companies

We live, as they say, in a global economy. To a large extent unit trusts are peculiarly British, based as they are on trust law. This does not travel well, particularly to continental Europe. Open-ended investment companies therefore represent something of a 'half-way house' between unit trusts and investment trusts.

An OEIC is an investment company and an investor receives shares in the fund represented by the company but unlike investment trusts these shares do not confer any form of beneficial ownership of the company. In that sense they are more like units in a unit trust. They are open-ended because the shares are sold by and back to the company depending on demand for them.

brilliant tip

The brilliant investor should consider the OEIC to be a more modern form of collective investment fund.

Investment bonds

Insurance companies offer collective investment funds as well. They come in the form of what are known as investment bonds. Strictly speaking these are life assurance policies but they do seem to have the attributes of collective investments because life assurance cover has a very small part to play in the process.

> life assurance cover has a very small part to play in the process

It is important not to confuse the word 'bond' in this context with corporate bonds, as described earlier within the fixed interest securities asset class. However, it is possible to invest in corporate bond funds within an investment bond 'wrapper'. Confusing, huh?!

The brilliant investor who buys an investment bond will be issued with a policy document and that policy document will form the basis of the contract between the insurance company and the investor. There will be a range of investment funds available ranging from low-risk cash-based funds to higher-risk equity-based funds. These investment funds may be managed by the company that provides the investment bond or, more commonly these days, external fund managers.

Each investor will have a number of notional units in the selected funds and these units will be the basis on which the investment bond is valued. As the price of each unit increases the value of the investment rises; as it falls so does the value of the investment bond. Investment bonds typically have initial charges and annual management charges but the investor should watch out for exit penalties which are quite common on these products.

> the investor should watch out for exit penalties

Like unit trusts, investment trusts and OEICs, investment bonds have no fixed maturity date: they can literally continue for the life of the owner and in some instances there might be multiple owners.

brilliant tip

When investing in an investment bond you need to keep a keen eye on charges. Many have overly complex and convoluted charging structures designed (it sometimes seems) to confuse the investor. A combination bid/offer spread, high allocation rates and exit penalties for several years after the investment is made usually have the net effect of no initial charge, but you need to understand the charging structure before you invest.

Investment bonds are sometimes criticised for the high levels of commission they pay to financial advisers. Whilst a financial adviser might receive 3% of your investment in a unit trust or OEIC they can receive up to 7% (or more!) from your investment within an investment bond. Ways to ensure that these exorbitant commission levels do not influence your adviser include paying an explicit fee for their services or asking them to take the same level of commission from both unit trusts/OEICs and investment bonds.

brilliant tip

Financial advisers have to, by law, fully disclose the commission they receive but all too often this disclosure takes place right at the end of the advice process. Demand clarity and certainty up front.

Pension plans

Pension plans are a tax privileged way of saving for the future. As well as income tax relief on the contributions which are invested into the plans, the build up of value within the pension plan fund is also tax beneficial; there is no capital gains tax to pay and most income produced within the pension plan is also tax free.

It will come as no surprise to readers to learn that a pension plan is simply a form of investment. What really matters is that the underlying investments are suitable for the investor. Typically pension plans are offered by the insurance companies but there is a growing demand for 'self-invested' plans where the pension plan owner exercises control over the choice of underlying investments.

As there are some quite valuable tax privileges there are also some restrictions around the availability of benefits from the pension plan and the shape in which those benefits are taken: for example, only a quarter of the pension fund is typically allowed as a lump sum. Investors also have to wait until they are 50 years old (increasing to 55 years old in 2010) before they can access any of the money within a pension plan. Thus pension plans are unsuitable for shorter-term investors who might need earlier access to their money. They should, however, play a role in your investment strategy for retirement planning.

> pension plans are unsuitable for shorter-term investors who might need earlier access to their money

How to choose the right place to invest your money

If you compare the various products described in this section you will find that they all have a different structure, different links to the various investment asset classes and different costs associated with buying them. You can choose to buy them directly or indirectly and with or without the assistance and guidance of an intermediary.

Here are some key questions to answer in deciding the best type of plan to buy:

- **Do you want capital growth, income or both?** Different plans have different objectives so you should choose an investment plan that meets your overall investment objectives.

- **If you want income is that now or in the future?** It is possible to defer the payment of income within some plans by simply asking the fund manager to retain the income within the fund. This almost acts as additional capital growth as the income can be used to buy additional units within the fund.

- **Do you want to be able to access your capital without having to wait?** It is important to understand the likely timescale of a particular investment. Even investments with no fixed timescale may impose penalties if you withdraw your money within the first few years. Look for any hidden penalties or charges before investing your money, particularly if you might need to gain access in a hurry.

- **Is tax relief and tax privileged investment growth important to you?** Never let the tax treatment of a particular investment option dictate your decisions. You should, however, take advantage of available tax relief where it fits your overall objectives and risk profile. More on this in Chapter 6 when we take a closer look at the impact of tax on investments.

- **Are product charges important to you?** Charges on an investment erode growth and/or income. If you can keep the costs of an investment down you stand a better chance of being a brilliant investor. You need to understand the difference between cost and value when it comes to investments. Just because an investment is cheap does not make it good value. Likewise, an expensive investment is not always a better investment.

- **What degree of risk are you prepared to take?** As we already explained in Chapter 3, understanding your attitude towards investment risk is essential before making an investment decision.

- **Do you want active involvement in your investment or do you want to delegate that to a professional fund manager?** This last question will guide your decision over a direct investment or a collective investment arrangement of some sort. Many brilliant investors happily combine a mix of both direct and indirect investments within their investment portfolio.

Summary

- There are four main investment asset classes – cash, fixed interest securities, property and equities. Every time you invest money you are making an asset allocation decision. This is what really drives investment returns. Getting good results from individual stocks or funds is just the icing on the cake.

- Cash is 'safe' from capital loss but still risky from a price inflation perspective. It can make a good home for the short term but is likely to produce fairly lousy longer-term returns when compared with the other asset classes.

- Fixed interest securities are the debt from governments or companies. Whilst the interest they pay is fixed they can go down in value. Some carry a greater degree of risk than others, and this depends on the financial strength of the company that issues the debt.

- Property is a familiar asset class for most investors. You can either invest in bricks and mortar or in companies that make their profits from land and property. The latter is a more risky option but has the potential to produce greater returns. Over the long term the returns from both types of property investment should be fairly similar.

- Equities are shares in the ownership and profits of a business. The rewards for investing in equities are dividends and capital growth. Shares are typically traded on a stock exchange with company performance and investor demand driving their price.

- To get access to an investment you can either invest directly or use a tax wrapper. There is plenty of choice when it comes to getting access to investments. It is important to consider the tax consequences of using a particular tax wrapper but you should not let this dictate the actual underlying investment decisions you make.

● There are several key questions you should ask before
  making an investment. By applying the set of questions
  described earlier in this chapter to every investment
  purchase you make you will stand a much better chance of
  becoming a brilliant investor.

CHAPTER 5

Alternative
investments

The term *alternative investment* is often used to describe investment options that do not fall into the mainstream categories described in the previous chapter. This would commonly mean investments like wine, art, gold and antiques. The term essentially covers any specialist collectors' item that might have an investment value.

It is also a term used to describe non-mainstream investment options like hedge funds and private equity. In fact, alternative investments cover just about anything, well, alternative!

> alternative investments cover just about anything, well, alternative!

In recent years alternative investments (or alternatives as they are often called) have started to find a growing place in the average investment portfolio. Whilst alternatives were once a pre-serve for either the very rich or very adventurous, they can play a part in a modest size portfolio for a more risk averse investor. Because they can sometimes offer spectacular returns they can be very appealing to the novice investor who does not always fully understand the complexities of this asset class.

Within this chapter we take a closer look at what alternative investments look like and what to watch out for when considering some of the more 'exotic' investment options you have available.

Using alternatives to reduce risk

Alternatives, when considered as a standalone investment option, often mean much greater risk than mainstream investment options. However, if you understand them they can help to reduce the risk of your overall portfolio by adding much needed negative correlation to the other asset classes you invest in.

Because alternatives tend to behave differently to more mainstream investments, they can play an important part in risk reduction. By introducing just a small amount of alternatives into your portfolio (say, 5% of your overall portfolio), the fact they behave differently to other asset classes has a risk reducing effect. If your mainstream investments are dropping in value there is a very good chance that your alternatives are going up in value at the same time. This is because investors tend to move towards alternatives at times of international crisis or market volatility.

Of course it depends a lot on which alternatives you invest in. A world stock market crash is unlikely to have much impact on the value of your antique comic collection, for example, but it may well push the price of gold through the roof as investors are seeking tangible goods to invest in. Gold is an example of an alternative investment which is viewed as a 'safe haven' for investors' cash in times of uncertainty.

> gold is a 'safe haven' for investors' cash in times of uncertainty

Another reason to invest in alternatives

Apart from risk reduction, another good reason to invest in alternatives is to make your portfolio more interesting. Very few people are passionate when it comes to investing in equities or fixed interest securities. Investing in art or fine wine can add a completely new dimension to a traditional, somewhat stuffy investment portfolio.

Because the range of alternative investment options is so wide, it is always possible to find investments that will interest you. Virtually any hobby can be converted into a profitable alternative investment option. In fact, having the detailed knowledge that often comes with a specialist hobby can give you a winning advantage when it comes to investing in alternatives. It might mean that you know when an investment represents good value because you will know what others are prepared to pay for it. Being able to spot a bargain and then realise the object at the real market value is a key component to brilliance when investing in alternatives.

The drawbacks of alternative investments

As well as having some positive attributes, there are some very real potential drawbacks when it comes to investing in alternatives. Some alternative investments have no intrinsic value. Art, for example, is extremely subjective because the value is based on current trends and tastes.

The performance figures associated with alternative investments do not always take into account associated costs. Because some alternative investments are not formally regulated, there is little in the way of investor protection so unscrupulous dealers can manipulate their numbers to make an investment look more attractive than it actually

> some alternative investments are not formally regulated

is. Alternatives can often have higher maintenance costs which really drag down the investment returns.

Beginners will find it very difficult to enter a specialist investment market and succeed at identifying brilliant investments. The more specialist the market, the harder it will be to do well without hard-earned knowledge and experience. You can pay an expert to provide this knowledge and experience but you need to ensure that their interests are closely aligned with your own.

The costs associated with some alternative investments can be huge, certainly more than those associated with more traditional investment options. These costs include insurance, storage and maintenance of the asset.

Hedge funds

Hedge funds get a lot of bad press but these are an increasingly popular alternative investment that has been around since the 1940s. Whilst once the preserve of the super-wealthy and institutional investors, such as life assurance and pension funds, this investment option is now gaining attention from mainstream investors who are attracted by some of the unique attributes and potential for spectacular returns on offer.

Big investment funds used only to allocate a very small part of their portfolio to hedge funds. This has all changed, with some of the biggest endowment funds in the USA (Yale, Harvard and Stamford) allocating as much as one quarter of their funds to hedge funds.

The term *hedge fund* describes a group of different investment management companies which share some important characteristics. These companies invest money in more or less anything that stands to make them money.

The word 'hedge' comes from a strategy often used by these funds where they can benefit from falling share prices. This allows them to 'hedge' against market downturns and still make a profit.

The typical aim of these funds is to produce 'absolute returns'.

brilliant definition

Absolute returns means investment returns greater than zero.

Most traditional investment funds aim to produce 'relative returns' by which they mean to perform better than the sector average return. This means if the sector average loses 10% one year they aim to lose less than 10%. An absolute return strategy should mean that, regardless of market performance, the fund will produce a positive investment return each year.

> the fund will produce a positive investment return each year

To do this, hedge funds use a wide range of investment strategies. Hedge funds may use one investment strategy or combine two or more to get the desired results. Unlike traditional investment funds they usually have a great deal of freedom and flexibility. This allows the manager to invest in a very wide range of different investment opportunities.

In fact, a lot of traditional investment funds, such as those you are probably already invested in, are starting to use some of these hedge fund investment strategies. Traditional investment managers are certainly starting to explore the benefits of certain hedge fund analysis techniques. There is really no escaping hedge funds!

These funds differ from traditional investment funds because they are typically uncorrelated to the rest of the market. This means their performance is not dependent on the market rising. A falling market can also generate profits for hedge fund managers because of the different investment strategies they are able to employ.

As well as being able to use these investment strategies, hedge funds will very often 'gear' their returns.

brilliant definition

Gearing is a term often referred to as *leveraging* in the world of investments.

Gearing simply means that the investment fund borrows money and invests this to try to achieve higher investment returns. An investment fund with higher sums of money borrowed is 'highly geared'. The more 'geared' a fund, the higher the risk because if returns fail to exceed the cost of borrowing then the fund performance will really suffer.

The drawbacks of investing in hedge funds

Whilst hedge funds aim to produce absolute returns it is important to remember they can lose money as well. There have been some notorious cases of hedge funds losing huge sums of money and investors suffering very badly. However, no two hedge funds are the same. Every hedge fund has a different level of risk associated with the strategies it uses so it is important not to group them all together when assessing investment risk.

The secrecy associated with many hedge funds makes it very difficult for the brilliant investor to choose a suitable fund. If a fund will not tell you which strategies it plans to use or fails to reveal recent performance figures, it is virtually impossible to make an informed choice.

> hedge funds may actually become a victim of their own success

Hedge funds may actually become a victim of their own success. Because of their increasing popularity there will be more cash chasing the same limited number of investment opportunities. This could make life harder for hedge fund managers over the longer term.

Getting access to hedge funds is likely to be the biggest challenge for the typical investor. Many are closed to new money and others have very high minimum investment requirements. The most successful hedge fund managers become popular very quickly and will close their doors to new money when they feel they are already managing enough.

Because a single hedge fund will often focus on quite a narrow market it is important to spread your risk by investing in a number of different funds using different investment strategies. This will give you a greater degree of diversification and more protection from the failure of a particular strategy or sector. Already in the UK we are starting to see the launch of funds of hedge funds where you can access a wide range of different funds, including those usually closed to new investors.

You also need to keep a close eye on cost and charges when dabbling with these funds. Hedge fund managers demand very high salaries (and astronomical bonus packages) which can really drive up their charges. They will often work on a performance fee basis, where they are rewarded more when the fund has a higher than expected return. These higher fees can really eat away at the fund performance.

Private equity

This is an alternative investment option with close connections to the world of hedge funds. It is a type of equity investment that is not traded in public so is not available to buy or sell on a stock market. It is also a way of raising money to invest in other companies, which may be available to trade on a stock market.

Private equity funds can be a very shrewd investment for a brilliant investor but they do represent a very high-risk investment option. There are a number of reasons for this higher than average level of investment risk.

The minimum investment required for entry into a private equity fund can be massive. For the typical investor this means committing more of your portfolio to a single fund and the resultant lack of diversification. It is not unusual to have a minimum entry level of £50,000 or more before you can invest in these funds.

> it is not unusual to have a minimum entry level of £50,000 or more

One of the biggest risk factors is the lack of liquidity. This means that once you have invested your money it can be very hard to get your cash back due to a lack of buyers or clauses within the investment company which prevent you from gaining access to the cash.

There are two main types of private equity funds – venture capital and mezzanine capital funds.

Venture capital funds

These funds typically invest in new companies that require funding to get started or grow at a faster pace. Because they are young and unproven businesses they represent a higher risk than investing in an established business. This higher than average level of risk means, in turn, the potential for higher than average returns over the longer term.

Mezzanine capital funds

These funds invest in more established companies that need an injection of cash ahead of being floated on a stock market and becoming a publicly available company for investment. It is more expensive for a company to raise funds from mezzanine capital than it is for the company to borrow money using more traditional options. This can mean that such companies are a slightly higher risk than those that do not need the money, but they should involve a lower level of risk than new companies with an unproven track record.

brilliant tip

To consider private equity as an alternative investment option you need to be able to risk large amounts of money and be in no particular rush to get your hands on the cash. Some private equity funds can tie down your money for up to ten years, so patience is most definitely a virtue if you plan to invest in this particular alternative investment option.

Investing in wine

Some hobbies can easily develop into an investment and wine is one of them. As an alternative investment option it screams class and sophistication, but is actually accessible to and affordable for the typical brilliant investor.

Most wine investment is conducted through specialist wine brokers or merchants, rather than buying direct from the vineyard. These brokers will guide you through the wine buying and selling process, in return for a commission of around 10% of the selling price. Because they are motivated by commission you should always take their advice with a hint of caution and check around to ensure they are offering you a competitive price.

> you should always take their advice with a hint of caution

Alternatively, you can cut out the middleman altogether and buy wine directly at auction. This requires a certain level of knowledge and experience to ensure you are buying good quality wine for a reasonable price. If you lack this knowledge or experience you may want to find a wine investment expert who is willing to accompany you to auction.

It is difficult to provide any guidance on the likely return from an investment in wine. Some sources claim that up to 30% a year is possible, but a more conservative estimate puts returns in the region of 10–15% per annum. In terms of risk, there are some risk reduction factors as the supply of wine is carefully controlled. This does not make investing in wine a risk-free option but it certainly diminishes the potential for severe capital loss over the long term.

You can buy wine at one of three stages:

- *en primeur* – before the wine has been bottled,

- around two years later when the wine arrives in the country or

- on maturity.

You are taking a bigger risk by buying wine before maturity but this also offers the greatest potential for higher investment returns.

brilliant tip

One big appeal of wine as an investment is that it is classed by HM Revenue & Customs as a 'wasting chattel'. This means that it is not subject to any capital gains tax when you come to sell the wine. The reason for this rather generous exemption is that the taxman views wine as an asset that will ultimately deteriorate in value, or at the very least get drunk!

Whilst wine is considered an alternative investment it is starting to make a greater impact in the world of traditional investments. Liv-ex (the index for the international wine exchange) recently started providing Bloomberg Indices with regular investment data on 100 different investment grade wines so it could include these prices alongside the main investment market figures. The availability of these sorts of data makes investment in wine a much more appealing investment option.

However, investing in wine requires more than just an investment motive. You should always invest in wines you are prepared to drink (and enjoy!) if they turn out to have no value in the future. Wine investors tend to be wine lovers for this very reason.

> wine investors tend to be wine lovers

Investing in gold

Gold, along with other precious metals, is an alternative investment option that appeals to many brilliant investors. It is considered a good place to invest if the world economy is having a tough time. Investors will often buy gold when the stock markets crash because it is viewed as a 'safe haven'.

Importantly, gold is a great diversifier in a bigger portfolio. Although as a standalone investment it represents a higher level of risk, it can actually reduce risk within a wider portfolio of more conventional investments because it is negatively correlated with stock market investments.

When it comes to actually investing in gold you have two options – you can either buy the gold directly or invest in something linked to the price of gold.

Direct investment in gold involves you buying it as either a bar or a coin. One of the most popular types of gold coin is the krugerrand. This is a modern one-ounce gold-bullion coin that is commonly traded. Because of the one-ounce weight these coins offer an easy price comparison with other gold investments. In addition to the krugerrand it is possible to buy smaller gold sovereign coins which carry a little more history. They are also considered to be a bit more attractive to look at.

Buying a gold bar is a bit more complex than buying a gold coin. Because they are bigger it can be harder to find a seller when you want to realise your gold investment. You also have to factor in the cost of storage and insurance. Not many home insurance providers will cover you for keeping gold bars in your house, even if you have a substantial safe available to keep them secure.

A good way to invest indirectly in gold is to buy shares in a gold mining company. This has the potential to work because when the price of gold goes up, so should the value of your shares. The main drawback with this option is that mining company profits are often linked to production anticipated years in advance. This means that a short-term rise in the price of gold will not always result in an immediate increase in the value of your mining company shares. Still, investing in a mining company requires a lot less cost and involvement than buying gold directly.

> investing in a mining company requires a lot less cost and involvement

Investing in art

Art is one of the most complex alternative investment options available for the brilliant investor. To succeed at investing in art you need specialist knowledge and a lot of experience. Due to a combination of a wide range of choice and the subjective nature of the value of art, you need to be an expert to ensure you get a good deal.

Art, as an alternative asset class, encompasses a lot of different things, including paintings, photos and sculptures. Actually buying art usually takes place through a specialist dealer or at auction. When buying at auction you need to be aware of something called the 'buyer's premium', which can add a lot to the price you offer to pay for the art.

brilliant definition

Buyer's premium is a term that refers to the additional costs added to the price you offer (the 'hammer price') to pay for a work of art at auction.

For smaller sums, under £10,000, the buyer's premium can be around 20% and this reduces in stages to around 10% for prices exceeding £60,000. This buyer's premium can quickly turn a sound investment into an absolute disaster if you forget to factor it in to your bid.

Like other alternative investments, you need to consider the costs of buying, storage, insurance and selling. Unlike many other types of investment at least art should provide you with a degree of satisfaction if you decide to keep it on the wall during the time you invest.

The key advice to always keep in mind with any alternative investment, particularly art, is to invest in what you really like. There are two reasons for this. Firstly, if you like the investment then there is a greater chance others will as well. Secondly, if you fail to sell it you can always keep it and enjoy the art for years to come.

Summary

- Alternative investments can be very risky on their own but the level of risk can be reduced when they are added to a larger investment portfolio. This is because they behave differently to more traditional investment assets.

- The drawbacks associated with alternative investments are substantial, but this should not stop the brilliant investor from adding a small amount of alternatives to their investment portfolio. Alternatives are great for making a traditional portfolio more exciting and interesting!

- Hedge funds have had a lot of bad press but are starting to become a more mainstream investment option. It is important to understand how a particular hedge fund works and what you are paying for the privilege of hedge fund management.

- Private equity is an alternative investment option with close links to hedge fund investments. It is an asset class predominately for the wealthy who can afford to tie up their capital for a long period of time and hope for spectacular returns if they have made a savvy investment.

- Investing in wine, gold or art requires specialist knowledge and experience. If you invest directly you need to consider the cost of buying, selling, storage and insurance.

CHAPTER 6

Tax and
investments

Tax is an inevitable, and unfortunate, consequence of brilliant investing. When you invest money and it grows in value there is normally a tax consequence. Income produced by investments is also subject to tax. Finally, when you die, the value of your investments gets taxed once again! There really is no escaping tax, but it is possible to minimise the amount you have to pay.

Within this chapter we will take a closer look at:

- the main kinds of tax you might experience when investing your money;
- how different types of investment are taxed;
- how to avoid letting the 'tax tail wag the investment dog';
- avoiding tax on your investments; and
- tax-efficient investment wrappers.

The three main types of tax on investments

When you are investing money there are three main types of tax to consider – income tax, capital gains tax and inheritance tax. Each of these can eat up a sizeable portion of your investments, if you let them. The brilliant investor understands each of these types of tax and how to avoid them.

> **Important note**: Tax avoidance is perfectly legal and ethical. I encourage you to take steps to avoid tax wherever possible, as long as you keep your overall investment strategy in mind. Tax evasion is illegal and doing anything classed as evasion will land you in a whole heap of trouble with HM Revenue & Customs (previously known as the Inland Revenue).

brilliant tip

When it comes to tax remember: avoid don't evade!

Tax on your income

The first type of tax to consider when investing is income tax. You should already be fairly familiar with this type of tax as you will experience it each and every month when you get paid!

In very simple terms, income tax is a tax paid on income. It is a relatively simple form of taxation applied to most forms of income. This includes income from investments.

When your investments produce any income, you are likely to have an income tax bill to pay. There are some exceptions to this and we will look at this a bit later in the chapter.

To work out how much income tax you have to pay you need to add up all of the income you have received during a single tax year (6 April one year to 5 April the next year). This includes your salary, income from investments and any interest paid on your savings.

some income is exempt from income tax

Some income is exempt from income tax. This is usually the case if you are self-employed and have spent any money on your business. You need to deduct this income from the calculation.

You can then work out which tax allowances you are entitled to. Every man, woman and child in the UK gets a 'personal allowance' each tax year. This is an amount of income which is not subject to any income tax. For the 2007/08 tax year this personal allowance was the first £5,225 of your income during the year.

The rest of your income is split into sections which have different rates of income tax applied. The first part is called 'lower rate', followed by 'basic rate' and then the rest is 'higher rate'. Different rates of income tax are charged in each band depending on the source of the income. Things get a bit easier from 6 April 2008 because the 'lower rate' is removed, leaving just a 'basic rate' and 'higher rate' to worry about.

Tax when your investments go up in value

When you sell an investment for more than you bought it for you have made a *capital gain*. This gain is then subject to capital gains tax.

You only have to worry about capital gains tax when you sell certain types of investments. These include property and company shares. You do not have to pay capital gains tax when you sell your home.

A capital gain is typically calculated as the difference between the buying and selling price of an investment. However, you can also deduct certain expenses from this figure to reduce the amount that is subject to tax. The cost of buying and selling the investment can both be deducted.

> everyone gets a capital gains tax exemption each year

Everyone gets a capital gains tax exemption each year. This is an important way of reducing the amount of capital gains tax you have to pay. For the 2007/08 tax year this allowance was £9,200. There are other allowances to consider which are available if you have held onto the investment for a long period of time.

The actual tax on capital gains is worked out by adding the capital gain to all of your other income. It is then taxed depending on whether it falls in the lower, basic or higher rate income tax band. In other words, if you already earn a lot of money you could be subject to capital gains tax of 40%.

brilliant tip

Capital gains tax is complex and you should seek professional tax advice if you think you might be liable.

Tax when you die!

When you die, the value of your assets becomes subject to inheritance tax, also referred to as 'death duty'. Everyone gets an inheritance tax allowance of £300,000 (for the 2007/08 tax year). This allowance is commonly known as the 'nil rate band'.

The value of any investments that fall into this allowance is free of inheritance tax. However, this 'nil rate band' is often quickly used up by the value of a house, leaving cash, investments and other assets exposed to inheritance tax at the full rate.

Assets worth more than the 'nil rate band' are subject to an inheritance tax charge at a rate of 40%. This type of tax can quickly destroy the value of investments you may have spent a lifetime building up for the benefit of your children, grandchildren or other relatives. Therefore, effective inheritance tax planning is essential to avoid this form of tax.

Other taxes to think about

As well as these main types of tax you may come across other taxes when you are investing. The most common of these is stamp duty. When you buy company shares or property an additional tax is levied. This stamp duty is based on the value of your purchase.

For company shares there are two types of stamp duty. On paperless transactions (when you buy shares on the internet, for example) you pay stamp duty reserve tax (SDRT). This is charged at a flat rate of 0.5%. For more traditional company share purchases (using a paper-based form) you pay stamp duty. This is also charged at a rate of 0.5%.

The only difference between SDRT and stamp duty is the way the charge is rounded up. For SDRT the charge is rounded up to the nearest penny. For stamp duty it is rounded up to the nearest £5. For this reason it makes sense to use a paperless transaction if the value of company shares is less than £1,000, to avoid paying unnecessary stamp duty charges.

Stamp duty is also charged when you buy a property. For property valued at less than £125,000 (as at end 2007) there is no stamp duty to pay. This is extended to £150,000 (again as at end 2007) if you are buying a property in an area classed by the Government as 'disadvantaged'.

For property valued at £125,001 or more the stamp duty rate ranges from 1% to 4% of the purchase price.

How different investments are taxed

Investments can be taxed differently. To make sure you get the best possible return from any investment it is important to understand how they are taxed. There is nothing worse than selling an investment, making a profit and only then realising you have a big tax bill.

Income tax comes in three different flavours – interest on savings, earned income and dividends.

Interest on savings

Interest on savings is subject to lower rate tax at 10%, basic rate tax at 20% and higher rate tax at 40%. It is usually paid 'net' by the bank which means it has already taken off 20% for tax before paying it to you. This means four things:

1 If you are a non-taxpayer you can reclaim the 20%.

2 If you are a lower rate taxpayer you can reclaim 10%.

3 If you are a basic rate taxpayer you have no further income tax to pay.

4 If you are a higher rate taxpayer you will have to pay another 20% (to make the total paid 40%).

From 6 April 2008 the 10% band will be removed, which makes life a bit easier. If you are a non-taxpayer then you can ask the bank to pay you the interest without taking 20% first. This saves a lot of hassle as you do not then need to reclaim the overpaid tax at a later date.

Earned income

On earned income (like your salary) income tax is subject to lower rate tax at 10%, basic rate tax at 22% and higher rate tax at 40%. From 6 April 2008 the 10% band will be removed and the basic rate tax band will change to 20%, in line with the rate for savings interest. Earned income includes rental income from property as well as income from pensions, employment and self-employment.

Income tax on earned income is usually collected by your employer using a system called Pay As You Earn (PAYE). This saves most people from having to worry about completing complex tax self-assessment forms every year.

> ## ☀ brilliant tip
>
> If you start to generate lots of investment income or capital gains you might have to start doing self-assessment. For some people this is a very good reason for keeping their investments as tax efficient as possible!

Dividends

Finally, there is income tax on dividends – the income from shares in UK companies. This has two different levels of income tax – a lower and basic rate of 10% and a higher rate of 32.5%.

Dividend income is all taxed in the same way, regardless of whether it has come from company shares or collective investments.

> dividend income is all taxed in the same way

When you get your dividend income you will also get a 'voucher'. This shows the amount of dividend paid and the associated 'tax credit'.

> ## ☀ brilliant tip
>
> Because companies pay dividend income out of profits that have already been taxed you receive a 'tax credit' to take this into account. It means that you do not pay tax twice on the same bit of dividend income.

The tax credit represents 10% which means that the dividend income you actually get in your pocket is 90% of the total dividend income paid. If you are a lower rate or basic rate taxpayer you will have no further income tax liability on your dividend income. If you are a higher rate taxpayer you will have to pay an extra 22.5%

on the 'gross' dividend (the dividend payment plus the tax credit). If you are a non-taxpayer you cannot reclaim the 'tax credit'.

How to avoid letting the 'tax tail wag the investment dog'

A common saying in the world of investments is 'never let the tax tail wag the investment dog'. This means that whilst tax considerations are important they should not come at the expense of a brilliant investment decision.

The easiest way to avoid letting tax planning dictate your investments is to plan in advance and not leave things to the last minute. The run up to end of the tax year (5 April each year) is always a busy time for investors and their advisers. Using careful planning means that you can avoid the mad rush to invest money before the end of the tax year, just to get tax breaks.

> you can avoid the mad rush to invest money before the end of the tax year

Your investment adviser will also appreciate having time to prepare their advice rather than adding you to the list of 100 other clients to contact before the end of the tax year!

Always keep your long-term investment objectives at the front of your mind when investing money and considering tax planning. If it helps, make sure your investment objectives are written down and refer back to them before you invest your money. If the tax break causes you to change your long-term objectives in some way it is probably not the right way to invest your money.

Avoiding tax on your investments

It is really important to remember one thing and one thing only about tax. Avoiding tax is perfectly legal. Evading tax is illegal and could see you end up in prison. There is a clear distinction between the two.

You need to be careful to understand when tax avoidance becomes tax evasion. It could mean the difference between a sunny retirement in southern Spain and a ten-year stretch in a dark prison.

The best tax avoidance means making maximum use of available allowances. A married couple has a great opportunity to hold investments in the name of the lowest earning spouse to avoid paying unnecessary higher rate income tax. This is often the first step to consider before moving on to more complex investment planning to mitigate tax.

brilliant example

For example, if a couple had £100,000 in savings that were paying gross interest at a rate of 5% they would be liable to £2,000 in tax at the higher rate. However, if the savings were held in the name of a non-earning spouse there would be no income tax to pay on the interest. This means an instant tax saving of £2,000 every year by making some simple structural changes to the way the money is held.

Tax-efficient investment wrappers

The three main tax-efficient investment wrappers are individual savings accounts (ISAs), pensions and venture capital trusts (VCTs). Here is a brief explanation of how each of these wrappers work and how you can benefit from using them.

Individual savings accounts (ISAs)

An ISA is often referred to as an investment but it is simply a wrapper that can be placed around an investment to protect it from tax. Think of an ISA like a raincoat with income and capital gains tax as the rain. By wrapping your investments in an ISA raincoat you can protect them from most of the harmful effects of tax.

There are two different types of ISA. The first is a stocks and shares ISA. As the name suggests this type of ISA can contain company shares but also collective investments. The stocks and shares ISA is not restricted to holding equities. It can also hold property and fixed interest investments.

Alternatively, you can have a cash ISA. These contain bank or building society savings accounts where the interest is paid without any liability to income tax.

The limits on different ISAs vary depending on whether you have a mini or a maxi ISA. This distinction is being removed from 6 April 2008 and it will then be possible to invest up to £7,200 every tax year within an ISA wrapper.

> there is no income tax to pay on investments held within the ISA wrapper

There is no income tax to pay on investments held within the ISA wrapper. However, it is not possible for investment managers to reclaim the 10% tax credit on UK dividend income. There is also no capital gains tax to pay on any capital gains within an ISA wrapper. For most people this is of little benefit as we all get an annual capital gains tax allowance we can use free of capital gains tax.

The main benefit of investing within an ISA is the amount of paperwork it saves when it comes to having to complete a self-assessment tax return!

Pensions

Since 6 April 2006 pensions are officially 'simple'. This is maybe an idealistic description of what remains a very complex tax wrapper, but they are certainly simpler than ever before.

You can invest as much as 100% of your earnings into a pension each year and receive income tax relief on the contributions. This income tax relief is based on your highest income tax level. This means that higher rate taxpayers get 40% tax relief on their pension contributions.

Tax relief for pension contributions is paid in two parts. The basic rate tax relief is added directly to the pension fund with your contribution. The difference between the basic and higher rate can be reclaimed through the self-assessment tax return process and the money is returned to you.

Once inside a pension your investments are sheltered from income tax, capital gains tax and even inheritance tax. You have to wait until you are 55 years old before you can access the investments inside a pension fund, and even then you can have only a quarter of the fund value as tax-free cash. The remainder of the pension fund has to provide an income and, unfortunately, this is taxable.

> you can have only a quarter of the fund value as tax-free cash

Like ISA investments, the 10% tax credit on UK dividend income cannot be reclaimed within a pension fund.

Venture capital trusts (VCTs)

A slightly more complex, tax-efficient investment wrapper is a venture capital trust (VCT).

These have been around for over a decade now and were created as a way to encourage indirect investment in a range of small, higher-risk companies. As such, they are a form of collective investment but structured as a company listed on the London Stock Exchange. This makes investing in a VCT a bit like buying a company share.

With risk comes the potential for high levels of investment reward. In addition, there are numerous tax benefits when you invest in a VCT.

- The income you get from share dividends is exempt from income tax.
- You get income tax relief, at the rate of 30%, on investments into a VCT.
- There is no capital gains tax to pay when you sell your VCT shares.

VCTs have to follow a very strict set of rules from HM Revenue & Customs before they can offer these valuable tax benefits. Having to follow these rules does mean that money invested in a VCT is occasionally returned to the investor because the rules cannot be met.

brilliant tip

Investing in a VCT is a high-risk and specialist activity. You should take professional independent financial advice before you invest your money.

Summary

- The three main types of tax on investments are income tax, capital gains tax and inheritance tax. You also need to know about stamp duty, another type of tax that you pay when you buy shares or property.

- Income is taxed in three different ways, depending on whether it is savings interest, earned income or dividend income from company shares. You might have to pay extra tax, be able to reclaim some tax or have no further tax liability. This will depend on your tax status.

- Tax avoidance is legal and is encouraged. Tax evasion is very naughty and could see you ending up in prison (or at least being fined). Understand the difference between the two and look for opportunities to avoid tax using legitimate allowances and exemptions.

- Planning in advance is the best way to avoid letting the 'tax tail' wag the investment dog. Do not leave your investment planning for the year until the week before the end of the tax year. Your investment adviser will also appreciate being given plenty of notice.

- The three main tax-efficient investment wrappers are ISAs, pensions and VCTs. These are not investments but wrappers which contain investments and protect them from taxes. The drawback of using a tax wrapper is usually less flexibility and choice over how you access your money. You need to think carefully about using these wrappers but they can provide important tax advantages.

CHAPTER 7

Becoming a brilliant investor

Once you understand the basics of investment, the relationship between risk and reward (and volatility), the different places you can invest your money and how tax impacts upon investment performance, you are ready to become a brilliant investor. This chapter takes a closer look at some of the ways you can get on the fast track to becoming a brilliant investor, starting with some words of wisdom from the experts.

We then move on to look at the three different ways you can analyse an investment opportunity. Making brilliant investment decisions gets easier if you use one (or more!) of these analysis techniques.

Reviewing your investments is the secret to being a brilliant investor over the long term. Brilliant investment decisions you make today may not be brilliant next year, unless you keep an eye on them. Setting benchmarks is an important part of this review process.

> setting benchmarks is an important part of this review process

Finally, we look at my seven-step 'battle plan' for becoming a brilliant investor.

Words of wisdom

Investment experts are never in short supply. Very often successful investors, such as those quoted below, will say something very profound about how to be a brilliant investor. Their collective wisdom is incredibly valuable to anyone who is thinking about investing their money or already manages their own investment portfolio. There is much to learn from these successful investors and their words can also inspire novice investors to make better investment decisions.

Warren Buffett

Warren Buffett is an investment expert, born in Nebraska in 1930. He is one of the wealthiest men in the world after making a series of brilliant investments through his holding company, Berkshire Hathaway. As recently as April 2007 he was ranked as the third wealthiest person in the world.

There are two brilliant investment quotations from Warren Buffett that every investor should read and understand:

Wide diversification is required only when investors do not understand what they are doing.

Whilst most investment advisers would recommend a wide spread of investments to reduce risk (a tactic known as diversification) this quotation explains that if you have absolute confidence in an investment you will avoid wide diversification. This is because, as well as reducing risk, diversification reduces the potential for greater investment returns.

> diversification reduces the potential for greater investment returns

Few investors will have the expertise, experience or dedication that Warren Buffett has and is able to commit to making brilliant investing decisions. For most brilliant investors it makes perfect sense to have a very wide diversification within an investment portfolio because of the risk reducing properties this approach provides. However, when you truly understand a particular investment it is possible to reduce this diversification, as long as you feel completely comfortable with the higher levels of risk.

Our favourite holding period is for ever.

Over a long period of time, investments tend to go up in value. Some will go up in value faster than others. The greatest thing about a very long holding period for investments is that shorter-term fluctuations in value will not panic or deter the brilliant investor. This is why it is often possible to take a greater degree of risk with the investment holdings for retirement planning than it is for shorter-term financial objectives. When time is on your side you can ride out the volatility in the market and hold onto an investment until the value returns.

Benjamin Graham

Benjamin Graham (1894–1976) was an economist and professional investor who taught Warren Buffett at Columbia University. He had the following to say:

Wall Street people learn nothing and forget everything.

Graham was referring to investors who speculate in shares that may or may not go up in value. His own approach was 'value investing' where the investor holds onto the investment for a long period of time. It is easy to forget past investment mistakes and learn nothing from these experiences when your mind is cast firmly on the next investment 'opportunity'. All brilliant investors should take this quotation to heart and ensure they have long memories when it comes to investments.

Jesse Livermore

Jesse Livermore (1877–1940) was a notorious investor in the early 20th century who made and lost several multi-million dollar fortunes. Whilst he did not always follow his own wisdom when making investments, he did have this very wise piece of advice to impart:

I never hesitate to tell a man that I am bullish or bearish. But I do not tell people to buy or sell any particular stock. In a bear market all stocks go down and in a bull market they go up.

This explains a fundamental rule of brilliant investing, often overlooked by investors who like to try to pick winning stocks or funds.

The vast majority of returns in a brilliant investment portfolio come from asset allocation – the market you decide to invest in – rather than the actual individual investments you make. If the whole market is going up, then your investment should go up with it. If the whole market is crashing then your investment is very likely to go down.

Peter Lynch

Peter Lynch is a stock investor on Wall Street, currently working with Fidelity Investments. He said:

In this business if you're good, you're right six times out of ten. You're never going to be right nine times out of ten.

Once again, an investment expert states that stock picking with consistency is simply not possible. Everyone gets lucky from time to time and investment selection is no different to real life in this sense. However, to find an investment expert or fund manager who can consistently pick winning investments is very rare, if not impossible. Refer back to the comment from Jesse Livermore and understand that brilliant investing is always more about being in the right asset class rather than being able to pick the best individual investments.

> brilliant investing is always more about being in the right asset class

Paul Samuelson

Paul Samuelson is a Nobel Prize winning economist and was a professor of economics at the Massachusetts Institute of Technology (MIT). On the subject of investing he had this to say:

Investing should be more like watching paint dry or watching grass grow. If you want excitement, take $800 and go to Las Vegas.

We often have clients asking us for an element of excitement within the investment portfolios we recommend, over and above the parts that are best suited to the level of risk they are prepared to take and the financial objectives they have for that money. Samuelson accurately describes how brilliant investing should be dull. It can still be interesting and engaging, but it does not need to be exciting at the same time. If your investment portfolio is exciting it stands a very high chance of dropping like a stone at any second.

> brilliant investing should be dull

Daniel Quinn

Finally, Daniel Quinn is not an investment expert, but he is a very talented writer. He said:

Many of the biggest and most far-reaching investments we make in our lives are investments that have little or nothing to do with money.

At the end of the day, being brilliant with investments is an important skill to have but money is not everything. Investing in yourself and your family is far more important than mastering winning investment strategies.

Investment analysis

Being a brilliant investor requires research and due diligence before making your investment decisions. Different investors make their investment decisions by analysing investments in different ways.

There are three main ways of conducting brilliant investment analysis – fundamental analysis, technical analysis and 'gut feel'.

Fundamental analysis

This form of brilliant investment analysis involves looking at the fundamental aspects of a potential company for investment. These fundamentals might include the company accounts, position with consumers in the market and the strength of the management team.

The fundamental investor is looking for a mistake in the pricing of a company share. They hope to exploit this mistake by investing in the share before the rest of the market realises it is undervalued.

Technical analysis

Technical analysis looks to spot a trend in the prices of a particular company share. It is used by investors who believe that fundamental analysis is flawed because all available information is already reflected within the price of an investment. Investors who use this form of analysis will say 'the trend is your friend'.

This form of investment analysis is commonly used to make decisions about the right time to buy and sell an investment. The trends can be used to help decide on a reasonable price to buy a stock and also to set the criteria for selling the stock when it reaches a certain pricing point.

Gut feel

This is a perfectly acceptable form of investment analysis which is used by many investors. It does not involve the use of complex charts or the analysis of financial data. Instead, the investor simply makes a conscious decision on the viability of a particular investment decision.

This form of brilliant investment analysis may not suit everyone but it should remain in place as a 'sanity check' before making investments based purely on statistical data. Even if the numbers are telling you an investment is sound you should apply some common-sense thinking before making your decision. Gut feel is a tool freely available to all of us that can prevent us from making silly investment mistakes.

> gut feel is a tool freely available to all of us

Combining all three

Brilliant investors do not restrict themselves to one of the techniques described above but instead combine all three when conducting analysis and before making investment decisions. The use of fundamental analysis to identify investment opportunities, technical analysis to get the timing right and gut feel to filter out any unwise investment opportunities is about as powerful an analysis process as you can find.

Review your investments

The worst kind of investments are the ones that are never reviewed. What might start out as a suitable investment runs the real risk of becoming unsuitable over a period of time. Brilliant investments are reviewed regularly in line with a set review process.

Do not be afraid to make changes to your investments if they are not working out as you expected. Reviews are an essential part of the brilliant investment process because they enable you to keep a close eye on what is going on. They should be carried out in a methodical manner and what follows is an action plan for you to consider using.

The review service from an investment adviser

You may choose to use the services of a competent investment adviser to help you review your investments. However, you still have some work to do ahead of any meeting you have with your adviser. If you want to ensure that you get the best value for money from the services of your adviser, regardless as to whether you pay fees or commission, then prepare and have some good questions to ask. For example:

1 Remind me why we chose these investments to begin with?

2 What are the goals of the particular funds?

3 How have they performed relative to other similar investments?

4 Have there been any changes to the fund managers since I first invested?

5 In your view do they remain suitable for my needs?

6 What alternatives should I be considering?

These are just six questions and there are many more that you might ask. At the very least going to the review meeting with your adviser armed with suitable questions will enable you to participate actively in the review process.

No advice

Of course you do not have to use the services of an adviser to carry out a review of your investments, you can simply do-it-yourself. If you do then you should still apply a methodical approach to the process and hopefully the following will help you to do so.

still apply a methodical approach to the process

Timing

How often should you review? There are no hard and fast rules about this but based on my experience once or twice a year is suitable for most people. Here of course I am referring to a formal review. It makes real sense to look at the progress of your investments on a more frequent basis, say once a month or once a quarter, but this can be less formal – say a look at how they are growing or declining relative to the general investment markets.

If each time you hear on the news that the FTSE 100 has fallen by 50 points this panics you into a formal review you probably have not got the balance quite right! Checking on the value of your investments on a daily basis is both unnecessary and unwise. This sort of review strategy is likely to lead to inappropriate changes to the contents of your portfolio.

You might time your formal reviews to coincide with the anniversary date of the purchase of your investments as this will tend to make calculation of growth rates easier. Of course if you have made various investments at various times you will need to choose a suitable date or dates.

What dates should you not choose for the review? Do not make it 1 January as hopefully you will still be recovering from celebrating a successful year of brilliant investing! Also do not make it 5 April because that will not give you enough time to take advantage of any end of tax year sensitive investment decisions. Also avoid birthdays, anniversaries and other memorable occasions because once again you will either be too busy or you are likely to annoy your loved ones who will tell you there are more important things to be doing!

Preparation

The beauty of personal computers is that you will be able to create a spreadsheet that enables you to keep a close eye on the investments you have. You may even be able to link the spreadsheet into 'price feeds' so that the number of units or shares you have is con-stantly being updated. Your adviser, or you

> link the spreadsheet into 'price feeds'

yourself, may have chosen an investment 'platform' from a provider and this will allow you online valuations and reporting.

If you do not have the computer skills (or access to someone who has – children are remarkably good at doing this sort of thing) then you may have to resort to a manual table and calculation of your investments. There is no problem with this, it just may take a little more time and effort.

Your investment 'spreadsheet' should probably have the following headings, at the very least, so that you can map out progress.

● Plan reference number

● Plan type (ISA, unit trust, etc.)

● Plan provider

● Investment amount £

● Investment start date

● Investment fund(s)

● No. of units or shares

● Current unit/share price £

● Increase/decrease % since last valuation

● Investment asset class mix (cash, fixed interest, equity or property).

It also makes sense to include a 'notes' column to record any additional information not covered under the other headings.

If you use the services of an adviser they should be doing this for you or at least helping you to design and create your own spreadsheet.

Setting a benchmark

If you invested £10,000 one year ago and it is worth £11,500 today (15% growth) you might well be pleased with that investment return. On the other hand if you rather hoped that your investments were going to grow at 20% then you might be disappointed. Either way there is something that you should note: 15% or 20% is not the *real* return. You need to adjust the return to take into account something called inflation. If inflation in the last year had been 3% then your actual investment return was only 12% because the purchasing power of your investment return is reduced by inflation. Investments should really always be measured in real returns because not to do so is simply a bit of self-kidology.

The first benchmark you should consider then is *inflation*.

The second benchmark to consider is what I term a *'what if'* benchmark. What if I had invested my money somewhere else? If you had done then of course you would have got a different investment return. Of course there are many other places that you could have invested your money and I am not suggesting that you consider all of them. That would be far too time consuming and also really rather pointless. No, you need to see if you had taken a slightly different approach what might have happened to your money.

When you first invested you probably created some kind of basic model of how much you should have in cash, fixed interest securities, property and equities. So a *'what if'* benchmark might say something like 'What if I had kept my investments in cash earning interest accounts?' If we take my example above where the return was 12%, and the real return from equities and cash in the last year was 5.5% (or 2.5% real return after

> benchmarks can help you to decide whether the return is worth the risk

inflation), then you can see that by taking the risk of investing in equities you have achieved a greater return on your investments to the tune of 9.5%. Benchmarks can help you to decide whether the return is worth the risk.

If you buy a copy of the *Financial Times* at the weekend there is a great deal of useful information in the Money section. (There is a lot of other very good stuff as well but let's concentrate on money.) You will find three APCIMS (Association of Private Client Investment Managers and Stockbrokers) benchmarks, for growth, income and a balanced income and growth benchmark. It might be well worthwhile comparing your investment returns against these benchmarks which seek to provide a useful measure for investors.

Individual funds

Within each investment product that you hold you will have an investment fund or funds. One benchmark you need to consider is the *sector average*. How well has the fund or funds you have selected performed against other funds in its sector? You might be quite happy with the 12% real return that you have received but if the other funds in the sector had all achieved 17% or more, how would you then feel?

If your selected fund or funds have massively underperformed the sector average you might want to ask, why? If you do not get a full and understandable (and acceptable) answer you might want to consider replacing that fund. Equally, by the way, if your chosen fund has outperformed the sector average you would be quite right to be pleased but you might also want to discover if the fund manager had achieved the performance by taking a bigger risk than their peers! There is no keeping some people happy is there?!

> reviews help to keep shocks out of the system

Reviews are important because they help to keep shocks out of the system. If you invest and leave alone that can sometimes result in both positive surprises and very disappointing shocks. The worst investments are the ones that are not reviewed so make sure you do have a review plan and stick to it.

The brilliant investor battle plan

Here is a simple seven-step action plan that we use with our clients when providing investment advice. It is effective because it is simple but it still offers a robust process for making and maintaining brilliant investments. When seeking professional investment advice you should always ask to see a copy of your adviser's investment advice process. Following a process like this is a great way of ensuring consistent results. Making investment decisions without a robust process is likely to lead to disappointment.

Step one – set your objectives

Before investing money you need to have clear objectives. Make these objectives as SMART (specific, measurable, achievable, realistic and time-bound) as possible. A general objective like 'capital growth' or 'income' is only a starting point. Link your investment decisions to specific objectives in your own life such as buying a bigger house, sending your children to university or a decent retirement. This will give you a yardstick to measure success and, if necessary, the option to make adjustments to your objectives, your investments or both.

Step two – think about risk

You should spend a great deal of time thinking about the level of investment risk and volatility you are prepared to take with your investments. Think in terms of the overall investment portfolio rather than individual investments. Some investments will have very risky characteristics when considered on their own but when combined with other investments the overall level of risk will fall.

Step three – select a strategic asset allocation model

Your strategic asset allocation model will dictate the long-term mix of your investments. It should be based on the likely future returns from each broad asset class. Keeping your portfolio invested in line with this model over the longer term is what will drive the majority of your returns.

Step four – make some tactical changes to the model

The strategic asset allocation model is all about long-term success. You can also exploit shorter-term returns by making minor changes to the longer-term model. This does not mean making wholesale changes and exposing your investments wholly to a single asset class because the short-term outlook is positive. It does mean changing your asset class mix by a few percentage points when there are clear market or economic indications that a certain asset class will do better than another.

Step five – choose a tax wrapper

Depending on your personal tax position and investment objectives you should then select a suitable tax wrapper. This might mean trying to shelter your investments from tax or simply investing directly and paying the price. This is the stage in the brilliant investment process where products are introduced to the mix. Many investors select the product at step one which is one reason they fail to be brilliant investors. Leave product to near the end of the process as this is where it belongs.

leave product to near the end of the process

Step six – pick stocks or funds

Now, and only now, you are ready to select the actual contents of your investment portfolio. Depending on the size of your portfolio, the level of risk you want to take and your commitment to the ongoing management of the portfolio, you can either invest directly or access these via collective investments. Choose investments at this stage that give you sufficient exposure to your selected asset allocation model. It is possible to add value to your portfolio at this stage, assuming you have given sufficient consideration to the previous steps in the brilliant investment process.

Step seven – review

As already described earlier in this chapter, reviews are an essential part of the brilliant investment process. Make sure you set up a documented review strategy when you make your investments rather than at a later date. This should include details of frequency and also benchmarks. Be sure to consider both relative and absolute benchmarks so you can really monitor the progress of your brilliant investment portfolio.

Summary

● You can learn a lot from the wisdom of investment experts. Some of the leading experts in the field of investments include Warren Buffett and Benjamin Graham.

● There are three main ways of making brilliant investment decisions – fundamental analysis, technical analysis and 'gut feel'. The most brilliant investors use all three in combination.

● The worst kind of investments are the ones that are never reviewed. Put in place a formal review strategy for your portfolio and make changes as markets and your own financial objectives change. An investment strategy might be brilliant today but it is unlikely to stay that way if you leave it alone for too long!

● Use the seven-step brilliant investor battle plan to ensure consistent results when you invest your money. This is the same investment process used by leading professional investment advisers. It is easy to follow and creates great long-term results.

CHAPTER 8

Get advice

Finding a brilliant adviser can be an important step in becoming a brilliant investor. The right expert can guide you through the minefield of investment choices. They can also arrange investments on your behalf, taking care of that pesky paperwork!

However, not every investor seeks advice before making those crucial investment decisions. Many investors are more than capable of making sound investments without any professional advice. With the rising popularity of the internet it is now possible to conduct investment research and buy investments online, often at a much lower cost than through an investment adviser.

Other people lack the knowledge or confidence to make their own investment decisions. They may seek advice as a 'route to the market', a way of getting access to investment vehicles and options not always available directly to the general public.

Finding a brilliant investment adviser can be a challenge. The information in this chapter will put you in a position of strength when forming and

> finding a brilliant investment adviser can be a challenge

maintaining a relationship with an investment adviser. With the right adviser you can turn every investment decision into a brilliant investment decision.

By the end of this chapter you will understand:

● the different types of adviser,

● where to find a brilliant investment adviser,

● how to pay for brilliant investment advice and what it is likely to cost, and

● what you can expect from your ongoing relationship with a brilliant investment adviser.

The different types of adviser

To be able to offer investment advice to the public, an individual in the UK has to be authorised and regulated by the Financial Services Authority (FSA). Anyone who gives advice about an investment without this authorisation can face a hefty fine and even a prison sentence. These rules and regulations should keep the cowboys in check but some people will still try to offer investment advice without the necessary authorisation.

brilliant tip

Before taking advice it is important to check out the adviser and ensure they hold the necessary permission from the regulator. The easiest way to do this is to use the FSA Register at **www.fsa.gov.uk/register**. If your investment adviser does not appear on this register then run a mile and do not take their advice!

There are two main types of investment adviser you can use. An investment adviser is likely to be either a financial adviser or a stockbroker, although some stockbrokers also act as financial advisers.

Financial advisers

A financial adviser helps their clients meet future financial goals and objectives by finding out a lot about their current situation and what they want to achieve. After making an assessment of the level of risk they feel comfortable taking they provide recommendations to their clients and help them build, manage and protect their wealth.

Since June 2005 there have been several different types of financial adviser in the UK – independent, whole of market, multi-tied and tied. It is important to know what sort of adviser you are dealing with as their status will have an impact on their impartiality and the range of solutions they can offer to you.

Independent financial advisers (IFAs) act on behalf of their client and have no links with investment managers, life assurance companies or other product providers. This impartiality means that they should always act in the best interest of the client and not be influenced by the commercial terms offered by product providers. As independent advisers they can provide advice on a very wide range of products from the whole of the market. They have to offer the option of paying fees for their advice and other services. Most continue to operate on a commission basis and will be remunerated only when they recommend a commission-paying investment product.

At your first meeting with a financial adviser you should be given a number of important documents. Their terms of business letter will set out the way they operate and the important protections you receive when dealing with an authorised financial adviser.

Since June 2005 they also have to give you a couple of Key Facts documents. These explain, in a reasonably good level of detail, their status, the services they can provide and the cost of these services. If the adviser works on a commission basis they need to let you have a comparison table within one of these Key Facts documents which compares their average commission

compare the services on offer based on value as well as cost

rates to the market averages. It is important to compare the services on offer from different financial advisers based on value as well as cost.

Stockbroker

A stockbroker is another type of authorised investment manager who will buy and sell investments, typically company shares, on your behalf. Stockbrokers offer three different types of service and it is important to understand what sort of service is on offer.

1 *Execution-only*

This means that the stockbroker will take your instruction to buy or sell an investment. Once you tell them what to do they will go off and do it on your behalf. This level of service is the cheapest on offer from a stockbroker because it does not involve the provision of advice. It means that you have to make the investment decisions and the stockbroker will make these happen for you.

Execution-only stockbroker services are now increasingly available on the internet or by telephone. Both of these options keep the cost down. In many cases it is possible to execute an investment trade for around £10.

2 *Advisory*

Using this level of service means that your stockbroker will give you some advice, but the final decision about what to buy or sell is left up to you. This is very similar to the service on offer from most financial advisers. If you opt for an advisory service your money remains under your control. You can say either yes or no to the recommendations on offer.

This level of service is more expensive than an execution-only service because the stockbroker takes responsibility for their advice. However, this additional cost may well be covered by the commission paid to the stockbroker when you buy the investments they recommend.

3 Discretionary management

The most expensive service available from a stockbroker is discretionary management. If you choose this type of service you will give your stockbroker a 'mandate' and then leave them to make the investment decisions on your behalf. It is more expensive than an execution-only or advisory service because the stockbroker is taking all of the responsibility (and risk) for their investment decisions.

> the stockbroker is taking all of the responsibility (and risk)

If you choose to go for discretionary management you are effectively giving control of your money to the stockbroker. This is suitable for investors who do not want the responsibility of making day-to-day investment decisions or people who simply do not have time to keep an eye on their investments. Before investing your money your stockbroker will have a detailed discussion with you to find out how much risk you want to take and what you want to achieve with your money.

brilliant tip

Some discretionary managers use model investment portfolios rather than create a bespoke portfolio of investments for each investor. If you are paying for discretionary management you need to make sure you are really getting discretionary management!

It is really important to find out whether your stockbroker is offering an execution-only, advisory or discretionary management service. As well as having an impact on cost, it will help you decide how much involvement you need to have with the ongoing review of your investments.

Shopping around for the right adviser

Finding a brilliant investment adviser can be tough. For starters, there are relatively few people in the UK who are authorised to give investment advice. The latest figures I have seen suggest that only 165,000 people, working for 28,000 firms, are approved investment advisers. Of course there is no guarantee that every one of these advisers will be a brilliant investment adviser!

brilliant tip

The best way to find a brilliant investment adviser is to use word of mouth. Speak to your family, friends and colleagues. If they have had a good experience with an adviser they will probably be happy to introduce you. By getting a recommendation like this you are sure to meet an adviser who has already done a good job for someone you know.

Failing a recommendation, you need to start shopping around. The telephone directory is full of financial advisers and stock-brokers. Start local and create a shortlist of five or so advisers. If you need to shop around then this next part will be quite time consuming but it will be worth the effort. Making a decision to use a particular investment adviser is very important so the time it takes to find the right person and firm is vital.

every brilliant investment adviser should offer an initial meeting at no cost

Every brilliant investment adviser should offer an initial meeting at no cost. Even before you arrange this first meet you should start to get a feel for the adviser:

- Did they sound friendly and approachable on the phone?
- What was their website like?
- Did they answer the phone within five rings or keep you on hold for 20 minutes?

Little things at this early stage can give you a good indication of how you are likely to be treated as a client in the future.

The adviser will use the first meeting as an opportunity to ask you lots of questions about your current circumstances, your financial objectives and your attitude to risk. Do not let them monopolise the first meeting. There will be plenty of time for them to find out all about you. What is really important at this early stage is for you to ask them lots of sensible questions.

Use the time you have together during the first meeting to ask some of the questions below. Check their response when you ask these questions. An adviser who looks uncomfortable or avoids a direct answer is not a brilliant investment adviser. They are likely to be more interested in selling you an investment product and earning a quick commission.

Top questions

Here are my top ten questions, along with the answers you want to hear, to help you find a brilliant investment adviser:

1 Are you independent, multi-tied or tied?

A brilliant adviser will explain that they are wholly independent and act in your best interests. A mediocre adviser is more likely to be tied to a limited range of investment providers or even a single company. They act for those companies to sell their products. Avoid them and insist on independent advice.

2 How do you charge for your services?

We go on to talk about paying for investment advice in the next part of this chapter. At the very first meeting the financial adviser should give you a copy of a document entitled 'Key facts about the costs of our services'. This will tell you how they charge for their advice and also the typical level of these costs. They will either charge by commissions, fees or a combination of both. Ask the adviser to be very clear about the costs you will incur when using their services and how these will be paid.

brilliant tip

An adviser who avoids giving you a direct answer to this particular question is not a brilliant investment adviser. Walk away!

3 What are your qualifications?

The minimum qualifications required to become a financial adviser are woefully basic, probably equivalent to a tough GCSE exam at school. If your adviser holds only the Financial Planning Certificate (recently renamed as the Certificate in Financial Planning) then they have demonstrated only a very basic level of technical competence which tests minimal investment knowledge.

A more robust test of investment knowledge comes in the form of the Diploma or Advanced Diploma in Financial Planning. These used to be known as the Advanced Financial Planning Certificate.

Never be put off by the letters after your adviser's name. Because of the different professional bodies available it is easy for them to pick up a whole series of impressive sounding letters from one exam. Ask them what the designations actually mean and what level of study they have been through to get their qualifications.

At the very top of the professional tree for financial advisers sit the Chartered Financial Planner and Certified Financial Planner qualifications. An adviser with either of these qualifications (or both!) has demonstrated a significant commitment to their technical ability.

4 What experience do you have?

Experience and qualifications go hand in hand. A highly-qualified adviser who has been providing advice for only five days is about as valuable as an

> experience and qualifications go hand in hand

experienced adviser with no formal investment qualifications. You need to look for a healthy balance of experience and qualifications. Ask the adviser how long they have been authorised as an investment adviser and the type of clients they have worked with in the past. You might also want to ask about their career before they became an investment adviser.

5 Can you tell me about your investment advice process?

brilliant tip

A brilliant investment adviser should have a clear and documented investment advice process. If you ask this question during the first meeting and they cannot give you a clear answer, walk away.

Having a consistent and thorough investment advice process is essential and will make the difference between brilliant and terrible investment advice.

6 What are your main areas of expertise?

No single adviser can be good at everything. Financial and investment advice is such a broad subject that you need to employ the right expertise for different objectives. Ask your adviser what they specialise in before you tell them your objectives. That way they will not be able to tailor their answer to fit your objectives.

If your adviser does not cover the areas that are important to you, ask them how they deal with advice in different areas. Some advisers will work with other advisers, either within their own firm or externally, to cover the gaps in their knowledge and expertise.

7 What is your approach to Treating Customers Fairly?

Treating Customers Fairly (TCF) is a relatively new initiative from the Financial Services Authority. It is a way of making sure that financial advisers consistently deliver a fair outcome to their clients. Ask your adviser what they think of the Treating Customers Fairly initiative to find out if they have embraced the concept or dismissed it as an inconvenience from their regulator. An adviser who says 'of course I treat my customers fairly or they wouldn't still be my customers' is probably not a brilliant investment adviser!

8 Do you offer an advisory or a discretionary management service?

Just like a stockbroker, a financial adviser can offer an advisory or discretionary service to their clients. A financial adviser has to pass a specialist examination and get permission from the regulator before they can offer discretionary investment management services to clients. Find out at this first meeting exactly what is on offer from the adviser.

> find out at this first meeting exactly what is on offer from the adviser

9 How often will I hear from you in the future?

If you are looking for an ongoing relationship with your adviser, rather than one-off advice, you need to agree on a contact strategy. Find out during the first meeting how often you will meet with the adviser and how they will keep your investments under review. Will they provide a regular valuation of your portfolio or even give you online access so you can check for yourself? Also make sure you find out if you can contact them throughout the year (by phone, e-mail or letter) to ask additional questions about your investment. This is also a good time to ask to see examples of their ongoing valuation statements and review reports. Find out exactly what you are likely to get!

10 Can I speak to some of your existing clients?

A brilliant investment adviser will be willing to offer testimonials from existing satisfied clients. Always take these with a pinch of salt because the adviser is likely to let you speak only to satisfied clients. Confidentiality can be an issue here, but the brilliant investment adviser should at least have some written or audio testimonials from their existing clients. You might even find these on their website or in their corporate brochure.

The cost of advice

There is no such thing as a free lunch. Investment advice costs money and brilliant investment advice costs even more. If you decide to get investment advice you will have to pay for it.

There are two main ways of paying for investment advice – commission and fees. In both cases you are paying the cost of the advice. The delivery of the payment to the adviser differs slightly, but the cost is always yours to cover.

Commission

A part of the charges you pay for investments usually includes a provision for commission. If an investment has an initial charge of 5% you should expect that this includes a commission of 3–4% for the investment adviser who sells it. On an investment of £20,000 this means that £1,000 is instantly swallowed up by charges and £600–£800 of that goes directly to the investment adviser.

commission is supposed to be transparent

Commission is supposed to be transparent. When an investment adviser recommends a particular investment they are required to tell you how much commission they will receive from the investment or pension fund, etc. This process usually works but unfortunately it comes at a very late stage. You do not find out the commission level until the recommendation is made and paperwork is ready to sign.

You also need to be aware of ongoing commission. The typical ongoing commission rate on an investment is 0.5% of the value of the investment each year. On that same £20,000 investment that means £100 a year goes to the investment adviser. This commission comes out of the annual management charge which is a charge you pay on your investments. Some investment advisers charge as much as 1.5% each year for their ongoing services.

always focus on value rather than price

When considering the cost of investment advice you should always focus on value rather than price. It is important to understand how much commission you are paying to your investment adviser so you can make a decision about value. Remember, a fool knows the price of everything and the value of nothing. Cheap is not always cheerful (over the long term, anyway) when it comes to investment advice.

Fees

The alternative to paying for advice and other services with commission is to pay a fee. This is agreed with the adviser before they give you any advice. It should be clear and explicit so you understand the precise cost of their services.

In theory, paying a fee for advice makes it cheaper. This is because the adviser charges everyone for their services rather than just receiving commission from a few when they are successful in selling an investment product.

Fees come in a variety of shapes and sizes. Your adviser might charge an hourly rate, retainer or project fee. Make sure you get some certainty over the size of the fees before you give your permission to proceed. Working on an hourly rate basis can lead to a very large invoice if the task takes a lot longer than expected!

> make sure you get some certainty over the size of the fees

You can pay your fees directly after being invoiced by the adviser or by asking the adviser to use any commission they receive to offset the fees. If you pay your adviser directly you should make sure they set up any investments on a nil-commission basis and ask the adviser to use the rebated commission to reduce your charges.

An ongoing relationship

brilliant tip

As a brilliant investor you should be more concerned with the ongoing relationship on offer from an adviser than the initial advice they give you. Building a long-term relationship with a trusted adviser can help you to make the best decisions with your investments, time and time again.

Ask your investment adviser how they would like to work with you in the future. This may involve annual meetings, regular valuation statements and review reports. You should find out what systems and processes they use to ensure the consistent delivery of these various services.

Also check with your adviser to find out what sort of news service they offer. Many brilliant investment advisers now run a blog where they will regularly post their thoughts on the investment market. Others offer a regular newsletter, by e-mail or post, which will help you keep up to speed with the investment markets. The quality of their newsletter is often a good indication of the quality of their advice. Find out if it is written in-house or outsourced to another firm. Your investment adviser should be able to write their own newsletter if they are a true investment expert.

brilliant tip

One of the most valuable ongoing services from an adviser is the ability to access them during the course of the year. Being able to use a brilliant investor as a 'sounding board' when a new investment opportunity comes up or you are unsure about the best course of action is a powerful sanity check. The ability to call on somebody who is already familiar with what you are trying to achieve and what your existing portfolio looks like is a valuable thing.

Summary

- There are a number of different types of investment adviser. Choose an investment adviser who will suit your requirements, either someone to execute your investments on your behalf or someone who will give you advice or take total responsibility for investing your money.

- Finding a brilliant investment adviser can be tough. Start by asking people you know for a referral. If you have no success with this then shop around and interview a range of different investment advisers before making your decision.

- Brilliant investment advice always costs money. Make sure you get good value for money by understanding how much the advice will cost and what you will get in return for these charges. You can pay for advice through commission or fees.

- The ongoing relationship with a brilliant investment adviser is as important (if not more important) than the initial advice they offer. Find out from your adviser how they will deliver ongoing advice and services.

CHAPTER 9

Brilliant do's and don'ts

nvesting is a very personal activity. No two investors will have exactly the same appetite for investment risk and the same objectives when it comes to investing their money. Using different investments is one way of making a completely tailored portfolio to suit your specific needs.

Regardless of which individual investments you select, there are some important brilliant do's and don'ts which can help you to ensure you make consistently brilliant decisions with your investments.

This chapter explains what you should always do when you invest money and what you should never do. There might occasionally be exceptions to these rules, but in general you will find it hard to go wrong if you stick to the following.

The brilliant do's

Do read widely

When it comes to your money, the more you know, the faster it will grow. Knowledge is power for the brilliant investor. Read everything you can find about investments to ensure that: (a) you know what is going on; and (b) you have a good understanding of different investment opportunities.

Do check the credentials of your adviser

Make sure you avoid getting ripped off by an unscrupulous and unauthorised investment adviser by checking their credentials before you take their advice to invest. The easiest check you can make is the Financial Services Authority (FSA) Register at **www.fsa.gov.uk/register**. Remember that the best con men are convincing and charming. Never assume that your investment adviser is the real deal. Always check them out first.

Do take a realistic attitude towards investment risk

It is important to take only as much risk with your money as you feel comfortable with. However, you need to be realistic about risk. If your investment objective is set for 20 years in the future (such as retirement) then you can take a higher level of risk because time is on your side. Over shorter investment terms you have to consider the impact of price inflation on more cautious investments. What costs you £100 today will cost you significantly more in five or ten years' time. You should always invest with this in mind.

Do keep some money in cash for emergencies

> it is rarely wise to invest all of your money

It is rarely wise to invest all of your money. Always hold some money back in cash in case of emergency. Doing this prevents you from having to sell investments at an inappropriate time. As a general rule of thumb you should always aim to keep between three and six months' typical expenditure in cash. It can take time to build up this emergency fund and you may wish to do this at the same time as investing some of your money. An emergency fund should be kept somewhere accessible but not too accessible. After all, it is there for emergencies and not as some sort of slush fund for when you really want to buy the latest handbag or gadget!

Do build a robust long-term asset allocation model (and stick to it!)

Long-term asset allocation is one of the most important features of becoming a brilliant investor. You might make small adjustments to your asset allocation model each year when you spot different investment opportunities, but over the long term your brilliant investment portfolio should be invested in line with your asset allocation model. As a brilliant investor you understand that most of the returns from your investments come from being in the right asset class at the right time. Picking the best funds or stocks comes a distant second. Get your asset allocation right and stick to it. The best investors understand the importance of asset allocation.

Do demand good value for money from your adviser

If you pay for advice or other services you need to demand good value. An adviser who is little more than a salesperson will not want to provide you with any ongoing service or support. If you pay your adviser on an ongoing basis (for example, through fund-based commission deducted from the annual management charge on your investments) you need to get something from them on an ongoing basis.

As a minimum, your investment adviser should offer a comprehensive annual review report, a face-to-face meeting where you can ask lots of questions about your portfolio and regular valuations. You should also be able to speak to them during the course of the year if you have additional questions or concerns. Many brilliant investment advisers now offer a regular newsletter to help you keep pace with changes in the world of investment.

Do expect to get higher returns when you take more risk

Risk and reward go hand in hand. There is no point in taking more risk unless you

> risk and reward go hand in hand

expect to see additional returns. When comparing different investment opportunities you should always seek to get the highest reward for the risk you are taking. The only way to get high returns is to take more risk.

If you are offered an investment opportunity with a promise of high rewards then the additional risks should be easy to spot. If you cannot see the additional risk you should treat the investment with caution. As there is no such thing as a free lunch, there is no such thing as a high return investment with low risk.

The brilliant don'ts

Don't believe everything you read in the papers

Nobody has a monopoly on investment knowledge. When reading about investments in the press always remember that journalists tend to take a strong position to make their feature more interesting and readable. They also want to attract advertising revenue and the focus on some newspapers may be there with this in mind.

There are many excellent personal finance journalists but they do not have to be regulated and do not need any professional qualifications before they write about investments. This is not to diminish the validity of what you read in the papers, but remember that it is just an opinion and very rarely hard facts.

Don't expect to receive free advice

There is no such thing as a free lunch and there is certainly no such thing as free investment advice. The cost of advice is often hidden within investment charges and then paid to the adviser in the form of commission. It is important to understand the cost of advice before you can make an assessment of the value of the advice and other services you receive.

An investment adviser who offers their knowledge for 'free' does so in the hope of selling you an investment product and earning commission. The best way to remove this bias is to pay a fee for advice and a separate fee if you decide to implement any investments. This may appear more expensive than working on a commission basis but it is often cheaper in the long run. It is almost always better value as you will be getting truly impartial advice.

Don't be worried about seeking a second opinion

A professional investment adviser will have no concerns if you choose to seek a second opinion. By doing this you are not undermining their knowledge or expertise but simply obtaining reassurance before you make important investment decisions. Making the right decisions about investing your money is important. Do not rush to make investments, particularly if you feel uncomfortable about any aspect of the recommendation.

do not rush to make investments

Don't buy investments based on past performance

If you make your investment decisions based on past investment performance, you will be disappointed. The top performing investments today are rarely the best in the future. It is difficult to consistently pick top investments based solely on past performance. Whilst past performance is a factor to consider, it should not be viewed in isolation when making investment decisions.

If you focus on getting the right overall asset allocation for your risk profile and investment objectives, the actual selection of funds or company shares becomes less important. If you chase returns and invest based only on past performance you will be disappointed when the investment fails to deliver the same results consistently in the future.

Don't try to time the market

Trying to work out when a particular investment market is at the top or bottom is a mug's game. If you try to buy investments at the bottom of a market, you are likely to see the market fall even further. If you try to sell your investments at the top of the market, it will keep rising!

> think long-term when investing your money

Think long-term when investing your money. Buy your investments and hold onto them for as long as possible. Assuming you have got your asset allocation right, this approach to investing money will reap far higher rewards than trying to time the market.

Don't risk more than you can afford to lose

Investing should not be a gamble. That said, never invest more than you can afford to lose. Investments can plummet in value, particularly over the shorter term. If you cannot wait for them to recover then you need to restrict your invested money to the money you can afford to lose. Over the long term you should expect the value of your investments to go up, but over the short term even the most predictable investment can do funny things.

Don't hide important facts from your investment adviser

Your investment adviser will ask you lots of questions. Some of these questions might seem quite personal. They will certainly want to know a lot about your existing investments. Tell them as much as you can. If you hide important facts from your investment adviser then their advice will be less effective than it could have been. They ask lots of questions for a reason.

Don't accept investment advice from people on the golf course

Everyone has an opinion on investments. In my career as an investment adviser I frequently hear about 'golf course investors'. These are people who invest their money based on tips and recommendations received on the golf course. Because these tips are often about recent investment success, by the time the 'golf course investor' invests their money they have missed the boat. Stick to professional investment advice from an authorised and regulated adviser. Leave the golf course for non-investment related gossip.

Don't invest in things you don't understand

By only investing in things you fully understand you significantly improve your chances of avoiding big mistakes. A confusing investment is far more likely to lead to you losing money than one that is nice and simple. Simplicity is bliss when it comes to investing money. By keeping things simple you also keep costs down. An invest-

simplicity is bliss when it comes to investing money

ment opportunity you cannot fully understand has no place within a brilliant investment portfolio.

CHAPTER 10

Brilliant tips

Y ou've read the book and now you are ready to be a brilliant investor. But before you go and play on the stock market or profit from property, here are ten top tips for being a brilliant investor. Keep these at the front of your mind every time you make an investment decision.

Brilliant tip 1 – Practise first and then risk your own money

Rather than risking your own hard-earned cash on the first investment opportunity that comes along, just pretend you made the investment.

There are plenty of investment websites where you can create a theoretical investment portfolio. Why not do this, give yourself some 'practice money' to play with and see how you get on before you actually invest your own money for the first time. This approach gives you the opportunity to practise your brilliant investment strategy before you see if it will work in the real world.

The longer you practise for, the more likely the results will be replicated once you start investing for real.

Brilliant tip 2 – Set yourself some limits and then stick to them

Whenever you invest money you should make a conscious decision to sell the investment when it reaches a certain limit. It is important to set both upper and lower limits. Decide on the minimum value you can accept before you will sell your investment or, in some cases, buy more at the cheaper price. Decide on the maximum amount of growth you will accept before selling your investments and taking the profit.

By deciding on limits like this at the outset you will remove a certain degree of emotion from the investment decision-making process. When an investment is quickly rising or falling in value emotions can easily take over. Rather than making investment decisions based on rational information you start to let your heart rule your wallet. Remove the chances of this happening by writing down your investment limits (if you have any!) and sticking to them.

Brilliant tip 3 – Don't invest just because everyone else seems to be

Herd mentality is common in the world of investments. Buying a particular investment just because your friends, family and colleagues all seem to be investing their life savings is a short-cut to disaster. People usually start to invest like this after the investment has performed well. Lots of people are suddenly deciding to put their money into the investment because they have seen the way it has performed in the past and they want a slice of the action.

Steer clear of any investment where this seems to be happening. Accept that it is too late to make a profit and you have already missed the boat. Even when, after a week or a month, the investment seems to be continuing the upward climb – stay away! There is a risk that the investment will become a 'bubble' and that bubble will burst. Don't let emotions rule your investment decisions. Steer clear of herd mentality when it comes to investing your money.

> steer clear of herd mentality when it comes to investing your money

Brilliant tip 4 – Watch those charges

Keeping costs down is a crucial part of being a brilliant investor. Over the long term it is the charges you pay to invest your money that will have the biggest impact on the end result. Putting your money into investments with mediocre returns is sometimes acceptable, as long as the charges remain low. Get those same mediocre investment returns but with massive charges and the value of your portfolio will struggle to keep pace with the interest you could have received on cash.

Brilliant tip 5 – It's advice, not an instruction

Investment advice is only ever a recommendation to take a particular course of action. The final decision always rests with you and you alone. Too many investors take the word of their investment adviser as gospel. Experience and qualifications are there to be challenged. Always dig beneath the surface of an investment recommendation, find out what work has gone into it and what has motivated your adviser to make that recommendation.

The alternative to taking investment advice is to hand over your money to a discretionary manager and let him make decisions on your behalf. If you are paying for advice, treat it as advice. Even if you are paying for fund management you should still monitor the progress of the fund manager.

Brilliant tip 6 – An investment that returns 200% in a year is never low risk

Take a realistic view about investment risk. Risk and reward go hand in hand. No investment opportunity offering three or four digit returns can ever hope to be low risk. If someone claims otherwise, then hold onto your money and run. Greed can be a powerful motivator when it comes to money so always stick to the fundamental rules you have picked up in this book. Question the wisdom of any investment adviser who makes dubious claims about the ability of a fund to make you a millionaire in the future. They are not living in the real world. You are a brilliant investor and know better!

Brilliant tip 7 – Keep good records

The best investors keep good records and stay well organised. If your investment records consist of a few scribbled notes on a scrap of paper somewhere, you need to clean up your act. Invest in a lever-arch ring binder to keep all of your investment notes and records in one place. If you are a computer whizz then set up a spreadsheet to track your transactions and portfolio. It does not need to be complicated, just a simple record of what you have, what you paid for it and what it is worth. It will become easier to replicate brilliant investment decisions in the future if you understand why you made them before in the past.

Brilliant tip 8 – Learn from your mistakes

Investors often make the same mistakes more than once. It is often said that they have short memories. It takes only a matter of years after a stockmarket crash to see the same investors piling their money back into the market in the same way. You can be different to this. If you make an investment mistake, accept it and move on. But before you move on you should spend some time thinking about the mistake. Why did it happen and what can you do to prevent it from happening in the future? It helps to make notes at this stage in case your memory is as short as the minds of many other investors. Keep a 'mistakes' page in your investment folder and refer back to it often.

> keep a 'mistakes' page in your investment folder

Brilliant tip 9 – Invest with a purpose

That purpose might be fun or it might be to give your family financial freedom. Whatever your reason for investing money, have a reason and remind yourself of it frequently. This is another great thing to write down and position prominently so you can see it on a regular basis. It really helps to focus the mind as you make those tough choices that come with investing your money. Having an end goal in mind gives you something to measure yourself against. It is essentially to have a yardstick so you can see what success (and failure!) looks like.

Brilliant tip 10 – When in doubt, buy yourself a monkey

As we saw earlier in the book even a monkey can outperform an investment expert when it comes to picking investments. Never take investing too seriously. As long as you stick to the basic rules your money will do more or less as you planned. Investors who take their money too seriously have sleepless nights because of factors well outside their control.

Investing should be fun and on your terms. If you find yourself lying awake late at night thinking about the investment decisions you should have made that day, change your attitude towards investing. Sometimes things happen that nobody could have predicted and certainly nobody can do anything about. If you get to a point where you do not know what to do next, get down to your nearest zoo and ask if you can borrow a monkey to make those crucial decisions for you!

And finally . . .

The world of investment can be big and scary. With the knowledge you have gained from reading this book you are better prepared than 90% of the people who start investing their money. You are in a really strong position to make brilliant decisions each and every time you invest your money. When you seek professional investment advice you will know what questions to ask and how to challenge the adviser.

use the lessons from this book to be a brilliant investor

Use the lessons from this book to be a brilliant investor. You now have the power to make a real difference to your financial wellbeing and meet your various financial goals and objectives in life. Every investment represents an opportunity to create additional wealth for you and your family.

If you want to be a brilliant investor, you can be. The time to invest is now.

Index